"Even when freshly washed and relieved of all obvious confections, children tend to be sticky." Fran Lebowitz

CHRISTELLE LE RU

Fresh Start

HEALTHY RECIPES AND FOOD TIPS FOR PARENTS OF PRESCHOOLERS

First published in 2008 by Christelle Le Ru Books Ltd

Copyright © Text and Recipes, Christelle Le Ru 2008
Copyright © Photographs, Christelle Le Ru 2008

Text, recipes, food styling, table settings and photographs by Christelle Le Ru
Graphic design by Vanessa Jones

ISBN 978-0-473-13439-6

Printed in China by Everbest Printing Co Ltd

Also by Christelle Le Ru
Simply Irresistible French Desserts
French Fare
Passion Chocolat

For ordering information and more, visit Christelle's website
www.christelle-leru.com

To ...
Noémie, Éloïse & Yohann,

with love from mum

Table of Contents

FOREWORD

Christelle is an inspiration. In between giving birth and raising three beautiful children, she manages to balance her life with eating healthily, keeping fit, working, and publishing books. This book, her fourth, is what Christelle is all about - cooking and family. As those of us who are normally rational adults know, getting young children to eat a variety of foods can drive one insane. The pages of this book are filled with recipes and ideas that will not only inspire you to cook, but your children to eat.

Christelle's goal is to provide ideas for easy-to-make, homemade, nutritious food that will fill up children without the need for expensive snacks and convenience foods. In my opinion she has done this perfectly.

A self confessed foodie, I was running out of ideas of what to feed my own children. Christelle's recipes have provided many ideas that were a hit with my children, as well as appealing to me as an adult. This is the first recipe book, in my vast collection, that has inspired me to successfully integrate a variety of fresh herbs and previously untried ingredients into my own children's meals.

In addition to the nutrition facts scattered among the pages of wholesome recipes you will find many commonsense but often neglected tips to help establish a healthy relationship between children and their food.

Victoria Landells
Nutritionist and Mother of two

Victoria is a New Zealander who now lives in Melbourne with her husband and two young children. With a passion for food she returned as an adult student to study Human Nutrition at Otago University. After completing her Post Graduate Diploma in Dietetics she worked teaching the practical components of foodservice cookery to university students and was the Food Service Manager at a University Hall of Residence. For the past six years Victoria has worked as a nutritionist in the area of food regulations both in the government and food industry sectors.

Savoury bits

Basic Nutritional Needs of Preschoolers

The basic nutritional needs of young children are similar to those of other family members. If you eat a varied and balance diet and ensure your children eat the same you will not have to worry. Little ones, just like adults, need to eat a variety of foods from all the food groups to ensure they meet their nutritional requirements of proteins, fat, carbohydrates, vitamins, and minerals. But of course the quantities needed are different. A good rule to follow for serving sizes for preschoolers is about one tablespoon of each type of food per year of age.

Proteins

Small children need to ingest some proteins. They help build muscles to keep them strong and healthy. Some protein can come from plants (for example, beans and lentils) but some should come from animals. This includes (but is not limited to) meat, fish, poultry, eggs, cheese, and milk.

Carbohydrates

Starchy carbohydrates also need to be part of your preschooler's diet. They burn slowly and therefore release energy over a longer period of time than other foods. This is ideal for active toddlers who can't afford to run out of fuel. Bread, cereal, wholegrain rice, couscous, and pasta are just some of the staple foods included in this category.

Fats

Fats are necessary, but not all fats are created equal. "Good" fats are monounsaturated and polyunsaturated fats. They are found in fresh and tinned fish (such as salmon or mackerel), avocados, and olive oil, as well as other sources. Be wary of the not-so-good fats, namely saturated fats (contained in deep fried foods for example) and trans-fats, the most dangerous of which are almost always present in heavily processed foods such as packaged snacks and biscuits, and are best avoided altogether.

Children under two years of age should be given full-fat milk and dairy products. It helps provide extra calories and nutrients that growing children need. Older children require about thirty per cent of their calorie intake to come from fat, as adults do. This is the time to consider introducing reduced-fat dairy products to limit their intake of saturated fat.

Vitamins and minerals

When it comes to vitamins and minerals, a child who eats a balanced diet with a variety of food, including plenty of fruit and vegetables, is likely to get all he needs. The more varied and the more colourful the food, the better. Try to choose in-season produce rather than the more expensive out-of-season kinds, which have usually travelled and lost some of their goodness along the way. There are many different ways to serve fruit and vegetables. Try to serve them as raw sticks for snacks, puréed, finely grated and mixed into a favourite meal, and so on.

Young children usually enjoy milk and get enough calcium from drinking milk to meet their daily requirements. Other ways to achieve the recommended intake include offering cheese, yoghurt, creamy rice, custard, and other dairy products. If your child can not tolerate dairy foods, non dairy sources of calcium include the bones from fish such as tinned salmon and mackerel and soy bean products.

The nutrient most likely to be low in a toddler's diet is iron. The best source of iron is meat as the iron is in a form that is easily absorbed. Other good sources of iron are pulses (such as kidney beans, chick peas, and lentils), wholegrain breads, and cereals that are iron-enriched. Serving meat minced or in casseroles will make it easier to chew for young children. Vitamin C will help your child to absorb iron from their meal and the vitamin C from the tomatoes will help your child to absorb more iron from his meat and vegetables. A casserole, pasta or bean dish that combines meat and tomatoes is a good idea.

Omelette aux pommes de terre

Herbs and potato omelette

Serves 4

Ingredients

- 2 potatoes
- 4 eggs
- 30ml / 1 fl oz milk
- 1 tablespoon freshly chopped parsley
- 1 teaspoon dill
- pinch of salt
- 1 tablespoon extra-virgin olive oil

Peel the potatoes and cook in the microwave oven for 10 minutes on full power. Insert a fine skewer in their centre to check if they are cooked and adjust cooking time accordingly (it will depend on your microwave maximum power). Set aside.

Whisk the eggs with the milk. Add the parsley, dill and salt and mix well. Slice the potatoes.

Place the slices of potato in a frying pan with the olive oil and cook over high heat for a few minutes. Pour the egg mixture on top and cook for a little longer until the omelette is just set. Cut into four portions and serve immediately.

This recipe makes a brilliant meal when time is scarce. It takes very little time to prepare and cook, requires basic ingredients, and even better, it is tasty and nutritious. If you can, buy organic eggs which are less likely to contain salmonella and always use them fresh, especially when cooking for young children.

Cake aux olives et au jambon

Olive triangles

Makes 15

Ingredients

3 eggs
55g / 2oz butter
30g / 1oz wholemeal flour
30g / 1oz white flour
55g / 2oz feta cheese
55g / 2oz ham
20 pitted black olives
½ bunch parsley

Preheat oven to 180°C (350°F). Grease a 20cm (8 inch) round tin.

Mix the eggs, melted butter and flours until well combined. Dice the feta cheese and cut the ham into pieces. Add to the mixture and mix in the olives. Pour this mixture into the prepared tin.

Wash and finely chop the parsley. Sprinkle on top of the mixture and fan bake for 25 minutes or until golden. Remove from the tin and cut into small triangular shapes. This makes an ideal finger food for little hands and can be served warm or cold.

These triangles are fuss-free and ideal to take out on a family picnic. Mixing white flour with wholemeal flour is beneficial as it adds a little extra fibre to your children's diet without over-doing it. Bear in mind that it is not recommended for littlies to have as high a fibre intake as it is for adults. The eggs, ham and feta cheese provide some protein while the feta cheese also provides some calcium. Olives are high in monounsaturated fat (the good variety) and on their own make a great snacking option.

Petits poissons

Salmon cakes

Makes 6

Ingredients

- 2 potatoes
- 1 × 210g / 1 × 7½oz tin salmon in brine
- 1 egg
- 1 tablespoon extra-virgin olive oil
- 1 teaspoon lemon juice
- 1 tablespoon parsley
- a few black olives
- 1 tablespoon tomato sauce

Preheat oven to 180°C (350°F). Grease a large ovenproof tray.

Peel the potatoes. Place in a steamer and cook for 10 minutes or until tender. Transfer to a mixing bowl and add the olive oil and lemon juice. Process into a purée.

Mix in the egg and parsley. Finally, drain the salmon and crumb with a fork, making sure to remove any bone. Add to the potato mixture.

Spoon out a small amount of this mixture and use your fingers to shape each cake into a fish. Use small pieces of olives to make the eyes and tomato sauce for the mouth.

Place the salmon cakes onto the prepared tray and bake for 25 minutes or until golden. Serve warm with a side of grated raw vegetables.

It can be tricky to get children to eat fish. Some love it; some just will not touch the stuff. If your kid is part of the latter squadron, mixing fish into a dish such as these salmon cakes may be just what you need to do. Fun to look at and delicious to eat, even the most reluctant child is likely to enjoy one.

Oeufs mimosa

Eggs "mimosa"

Makes 8

Ingredients

    4 eggs
    1 tablespoon tomato sauce
    30g / 1oz cheddar cheese
    salt and pepper

Bring a saucepan filled with water to the boil and cook the eggs for 10 minutes. Leave to cool.

Shell and halve the eggs. Remove the yolks and place the empty egg whites on a plate.

Place the yolks in a mixing bowl. Crumb and mix with the tomato sauce. Season lightly with salt and pepper.

Use this mixture to fill the egg whites. Sprinkle with grated cheese and serve chilled with a slice of toast and some shredded lettuce.

A recipe can not get much simpler than this one. At the same time, this dish is full of protein and makes a great light meal for a child, and it is more exciting to eat than a plain hard-boiled egg. The lettuce or other raw vegetables may sometimes be left almost untouched but it is good practice to always offer a variety of nutritious foods. Even if your children do not show much enthusiasm initially it is important to create opportunities for them to try out these less-favoured foods. After a while, they should gradually start enjoying their side salad, like their parents!

Basic Nutritional Needs of Preschoolers - continued

Foods to limit

Limit sugary foods that provide few nutrients and can contribute to obesity and tooth decay. It is fine to offer dessert, but go for naturally sweet foods such as fruit that will contribute vitamins, or natural yoghurt, which is high in much-needed calcium. Keep the seriously decadent desserts for special occasions such as birthdays, and keep portion sizes under control.

As for convenience foods, although many frozen, tinned, or chilled foods are nutritionally sound, be aware that many also contain a lot of salt, which puts a strain on a little child's kidneys. Fast foods are often high in salt, sugar, and fat, but low in nutrients, while processed foods generally contain chemical preservatives, colourings, and flavourings that you may prefer to avoid feeding your toddler.

Drinks

It is very important that your children drink enough water, as it is needed to regulate body functions. As a percentage of body weight, children have more water in their bodies than adults. To stop them from becoming dehydrated, make sure you offer plenty of drinks to your preschooler throughout the day. This being said, a child's stomach is small, so they will be less likely to eat their meals properly if they fill up on drinks. As for anything, moderation is the key.

To quench thirst, water is the drink of choice for a small child – and it is cheap too. You can make water more appealing by serving it with slices of lemon or orange, or popping in a couple of home-made flavoured ice-cubes. To make ice-cubes, fill ice-cube trays with juiced oranges or watermelons, puréed kiwifruit or rockmelons, or chopped pieces of apples or pears topped up with water, and freeze.

Milk is important for young children. They should have two to three serves of dairy a day. One or more glasses of milk is an easy way to get one or more serves. Health professionals generally advise that children under two be given whole milk rather than its skimmed or semi-skimmed counterpart.

Avoid sweet drinks such as juice and soft drinks. They are bad for the teeth and may promote tooth decay if consumed too often. Moreover, serving sweetened drinks on a regular basis can accustom your children to sweet things. The best thing to give to a thirsty child is water. If serving fruit juice, it is always best to take a few minutes to squeeze a couple of fresh oranges. If you do serve bottled juice, dilute it with equal amounts of water. To help your children drink enough, remember to offer water with all meals and snacks, and don't forget to carry a water bottle with you when you go out.

Snacks

Young children need to eat frequently. They have small stomachs, and it is difficult for them to cover their nutritional needs in just three meals. They really need snacks to keep them going between meals, so you should offer a mid-morning and mid-afternoon snack every day. Use snack times to help your children fill out their daily requirements of nutrients. Snacks should not be empty calories: preschoolers eat small quantities and have no room for calories that are free of nutrients.

Keep a stock of healthy snacks at home so you can quickly throw a couple in your bag when you go out in a rush. Try to avoid crisps and sweets as much as possible. Instead offer healthier alternatives such as bananas, wholemeal bread, fruit bread, cheese cubes with rice crackers, dried fruit, fresh fruit slices, a tub of plain yoghurt with fresh fruit and/or honey, oatmeal biscuits, or vegetable sticks with a dip.

Experts agree that the best way to ensure your children meets their daily needs is to give them three meals and two snacks a day. Provide nutritious food to increase the chances of your children eating a healthy, balanced diet.

Velouté de pommes de terre

Cream of potato soup

Serves 4

Ingredients

2 potatoes
1 shallot
1 clove garlic
¼ lettuce
1 bay leaf
250ml / 9fl oz milk
120ml / 4fl oz unsweetened
condensed milk
70g / 2½oz gruyere

Peel the potatoes, shallot and garlic. Wash the lettuce thoroughly and shred. Cut the potatoes into chunks. Place all these vegetables along with the bay leaf in a steamer and cook for 10 minutes.

Discard the bay leaf and transfer the vegetables into a mixing bowl. Add the milk, condensed milk and process into a purée. Serve hot with a slice of wholemeal bread and grated gruyere.

This simple dish is packed full with nutrients and is heart-warming in the cooler months. Condensed milk increases the calcium content of this meal and makes this soup creamy but is lower in fat than cream.

Sushi

Sushi

Makes 35

Ingredients

- 360g / 12½oz sushi rice
- 1l / 34fl oz water
- 1 packet sushi flavouring
- 7 sushi nori (seaweed sheets)
- 1 x 185g / 1 x 6½oz tin tuna in brine
- 2 tablespoons mayonnaise
- 2 large lettuce leaves
- ¼ telegraph cucumber
- 1 carrot
- ½ avocado

Bring the water to the boil in a large saucepan. Cook the rice uncovered for 40 minutes or until all the water has been absorbed and the rice is tender. Add some water if necessary. Mix the sushi flavouring into the hot rice. Leave to cool.

Peel and grate the carrot. Peel and halve the cucumber, and cut lengthways into fine sticks. Remove the flesh from the avocado and cut into small pieces. Shred the lettuce. Drain the tuna and mix with the mayonnaise.

Place one sushi nori on a sushi mat and dampen with wet fingers. Place a large spoonful of cooked rice on the sushi nori. Flatten with your hands to finely cover the sushi nori, leaving 1cm / ½ inch free on either side. Place a little tuna at one end of the rice. Top with a piece of each prepared vegetable. Roll up. Repeat until all the ingredients have been used up. Cut each sushi roll into 5 pieces and place on a large serving plate with light soy sauce and marinated ginger.

Finger food by excellence, sushi is a favourite among many children. Very versatile, it can be made with many different fillings to accommodate all tastes. Eaten cold, sushi makes a great summer dish and can easily be taken on a picnic. Just make sure to keep refrigerated, transport in a chiller pack and eat fresh.

Pains au thon

Tuna melts

Makes 4

Ingredients

2 English muffins
1 x 185g / 1 x 6½oz tin tuna in brine
½ lemon, juiced
2 tablespoons Greek-style yoghurt
2 tablespoons tomato sauce
55g / 2oz cheddar cheese
1 tablespoon coriander leaves
salt and pepper

Preheat oven to 200°C (400°F). Place the drained tuna in a bowl and crumb. Mix in the lemon juice, yoghurt and tomato sauce. Season lightly with salt and pepper.

Toast the English muffins and split up. Place on an ovenproof tray and spread a quarter of the tuna mixture on top of each muffin split. Sprinkle with grated cheese.

Place under the grill in the oven for a couple of minutes until the cheese has melted. Sprinkle with the finely chopped coriander leaves and serve immediately.

Children will love this café-style dish which provides carbs and proteins. Serve it with a selection of raw vegetables to further boost the vitamin and mineral contents of this meal. To vary the flavour, you can also substitute the tuna for cooked minced beef or chicken strips.

Flan de courgettes

Courgette flan

Serves 6

Ingredients

  500g / 1lb 2oz courgettes
  10 eggs
  150ml / 5fl oz milk
  100g / 3½oz Gruyere cheese
  salt and pepper
  2 tablespoons fresh parsley

Preheat oven to 150°C (300°F). Grease a 23cm (9 inch) round ovenproof dish.

Wash the courgettes and cut off both ends. Finely slice. Sprinkle with salt and place in a colander. Leave for 15 minutes.

Rinse and dry the slices of courgette. Place at the bottom of the prepared dish.

Beat the eggs with the milk. Season with salt and pepper. Pour over the courgette slices and sprinkle with the grated cheese and chopped parsley.

Bake for 30 minutes or until the eggs are set and the top is golden. Serve immediately.

Courgettes are a summer vegetable of choice. They are really easy for your kids to grow in their own vege patch. Combined with eggs, cheese and herbs like in this recipe, they make a satisfying and delicious meal packed with proteins and calcium. This dish will appeal not just to children but to the whole family.

Lasagnes végétariennes

Vegetarian lasagna

Serves 8

Ingredients

- 1 pack lasagna sheets
- 1 onion
- 2 mushrooms
- 1½ yellow capsicum
- 1 broccoli head
- 2 carrots
- 2 tablespoons extra-virgin olive oil
- 1 tablespoon freshly chopped parsley
- 1 × 140g / 1 × 5oz tin tomato paste
- 2 × 410g / 2 × 14½oz tin tomatoes
- 3 eggs
- 300ml / 10fl oz milk
- 100g / 3½oz grated cheese

Preheat oven to 180°C (350°F). Grease a deep 35 × 27cm (14 × 11 inch) rectangular oven dish. Peel and finely chop the onion. Clean and slice the mushrooms. Halve and remove the seeds from the capsicums. Cut into strips. Peel and grate the carrots. Cut the broccoli head into small chunks and place all the vegetables in a frying pan with the olive oil.

Cover and cook over medium heat for 10 minutes. Mix in the parsley and tomato paste. Blend the tinned tomatoes in a mixing bowl and add to the vegetables.

Place a layer of lasagne sheets at the bottom of the prepared dish and cover with half the vegetable mixture. Repeat. Finish with a layer of lasagne sheets and top with the beaten eggs and milk. Sprinkle with cheese. Bake for 40 minutes and enjoy.

This is another family favourite that will be enjoyed just as much by the adults as by the children. If your child is under one, you may like to process a small amount of lasagne with an electric blender for him. This technique takes little time and allows even the youngest members of the family to enjoy the same meals as everybody else. The topping may be substituted with a cheese sauce if desired.

Snacks au jambon et au fromage

Cheese and ham snacks

Makes 20

Ingredients

- 12 crackers
- 2 slices ham
- 30g / 1oz cream cheese
- 30g / 1oz feta cheese
- 5cm / 2in cucumber
- a few pitted black olives
- ½ tomato

Clean and slice the cucumber. Cut the ham into small pieces. Halve the olives. Cut the tomato and the feta cheese into small pieces.

Spread the cream cheese over the crackers and top each one with a olive half.

Top each slice of cucumber with a piece of ham, a piece of feta cheese and a piece of tomato.

Place the cucumber slices and crackers on a plate and serve as a nutritious snack.

Use everyday food to create simple yet healthy snacks. Mix a range of fresh, raw vegetables, cheeses, ham or sliced boiled eggs and some crispy bread or rice crackers to make a colourful, attractive platter for your kids. Ideal for a picnic or a party, these snacks can be made in large quantities in very little time. Just use your imagination and vary the ingredients and presentation as desired.

Encouraging Healthy Eating

It is never too early to teach children good eating habits that will develop into lifelong patterns. Habits learnt during preschool years are likely to remain when children grow into adulthood. Therefore it is all the more important to use this time to encourage a healthy attitude towards food, as well as a taste for healthy food. Teaching your children that eating a balanced diet is part of a healthy lifestyle is a step in the right direction.

Setting a positive example

The greatest influence you have on your children is through your actions, not your words. Hence it is important to eat well yourself. Children watch what you are eating, so to be a good role model for them, try to give up some of the junk food you are used to having in your pantry such as packets of biscuits or bags of crisps. This could make a big difference for your children, and it is most likely to have a positive effect on you too!

To teach your child how to have a positive relationship with food, you need to have a healthy attitude yourself. Make sure that you are not fixated on junk food and that you do not place too much importance on food in general. This may help your child later on by stopping them from obsessing about food and from potentially developing an eating disorder.

Choosing healthier alternatives

To give traditional recipes a healthier twist, substitute natural yoghurt for cream, add some grated fruit and use good quality ingredients in smaller quantities. For example, rather than using baking chocolate, which often contains hydrogenated vegetable oils or trans-fats, use good quality dark chocolate.

Learn to compromise. If your children are adamant about sweetened yoghurt, a good compromise could be buying unsweetened natural yoghurt and mixing in a small amount of liquid honey or homemade jam yourself. This is healthier than opting for the ready-made fruit yoghurts with additives, colourings, flavourings, and preservatives.

Limit sweets, salty and fatty snacks, and soft drinks, so that your children do not develop an unhealthy taste for such food. Instead aim to give them a love for fruit and vegetables early on. One way to achieve this is by offering these foods often and by preparing and presenting them in the right way. It can take many attempts to get a toddler to try out a new food – especially if it doesn't come out of a packet and isn't drizzled in chocolate. Children tend to model themselves on their parents so again, it helps if they see you eating it too.

Treating food as fuel

Don't always insist on a clean plate as it may lead your children to ignore their own internal hunger cues. Keep in mind that young children are able to regulate their food intake according to their own needs – you want to keep it this way. Encouraging children to listen to their tummy is preferable when it comes to the long-term goal of helping them develop a healthy relationship with food.

It can be tempting to promise an ice-cream to get your toddler to eat his spinach, but in the long run this is just not the way to go. By using food as a bribe, you are simply teaching your children that some foods are more desirable than others, and encouraging them to keep on arguing at mealtimes in order to get treats. This may also lead to problems later on. Every parent knows it is impossible not to bribe at some point but only ever do so as a last resort – when you are just too desperate and too tired to use a more suitable tactic. Food is about nutrition, not power struggles!

Tarte aux épinards, jambon et potiron

Spinach, ham and pumpkin tart

Serves 8

Ingredients

Shortcrust pastry
1 egg
125g / 4½oz butter
100g / 3½oz wholemeal flour
125g / 4½oz white flour

Filling
200g / 7oz pumpkin flesh
1 bunch spinach
200g / 7oz ham
3 eggs
2 tablespoons milk
55g / 2oz Gouda cheese

Preheat oven to 200°C (400°F). Grease a 23cm (9 inch) round baking tin. To make the shortcrust pastry, mix the egg with the melted butter. Add the flours and mix well.

Press the pastry with your fingers into the base and sides of the prepared tin. Prick all over with a fork and chill for 15 minutes.

Cut the pumpkin flesh into chunks and cook in a steamer for five minutes. Process into a purée with a blender. Wash the spinach and place in a frying pan with a little water. Cover and cook over medium heat for five minutes.

Cut the ham into pieces. Whisk the eggs lightly with the milk. Mix in the spinach, pumpkin and pieces of ham.

Fan bake the pastry for 10 minutes. Drop the oven temperature to 180°C (350°F). Pour the egg and vegetable mixture over the pastry base and sprinkle with grated Gouda cheese. Fan bake for 25 minutes or until just set and enjoy warm or cold.

Being creative and using the right combination of ingredients is paramount. By mixing a couple of fresh vegetables with old favourites – in this case ham and cheese – and presenting them in an appealing way, your children are more likely not only to taste your food but actually eat it too. The delicious crunchy pastry used in this recipe only takes a few minutes to make so it is well worth making your own. The use of wholemeal flour makes it a healthier alternative to ready-made frozen pastry as it will increase the fibre content of the meal.

Mini-pizzas à la crème de fromage

Cream cheese mini-pizzas

Makes 4

Ingredients

4 plain mini-pizza bases
100g / 3½oz skinless chicken breast
1 tablespoon extra-virgin olive oil
100g / 3½oz plain cream cheese
55g / 2oz feta cheese
4 tablespoons tomato paste
1 tablespoon freshly chopped parsley

Preheat oven to 200°C (400°F). Mince the chicken and cook with the oil in a frying pan over high heat until cooked through. Turn off the heat and mix in the cream cheese. Stir until melted. Cut the feta cheese into small pieces.

Spread the tomato paste over the pizza bases Top with the chicken mixture and feta cheese. Sprinkle with the parsley and bake for 15 minutes or until crispy. Serve immediately with a side salad.

Pizza is universally liked by children. These cute little pizzas are made using ready-made bases but of course make your own if you have the time and inclination. Cover the bases with a homemade topping such as the one suggested here or any other favourite foods. Beef or ham could be used in place of chicken, minced to make the meat easier to chew.

Macédoine au jambon

Ham and vegetable rolls

Makes 8

Ingredients

8 slices ham
½ × 340g / ½ × 12oz tin peas
½ × 340g / ½ × 12oz tin green beans
½ × 340g / ½ × 12oz tin baby carrots
½ × 340g / ½ × 12oz tin corn kernels

Beetroot sauce

3 tablespoons Greek-style yoghurt
2 tablespoons cooked and diced
beetroot
salt and pepper

To make the sauce, process the beetroot
with the yoghurt. Season with salt and
pepper.

Drain all of the vegetables and mix well.
Mix in a little of the beetroot sauce and
set the remaining sauce aside.

Place the slices of ham on a plate and
place a spoonful of the vegetable mixture
at one end of each slice. Roll up and serve
chilled with some extra beetroot sauce.

This is something my mum made for my sister and I when we were little and as
simple as it is, we really enjoyed it. It makes a very quick and healthy lunch idea
and is made with canned vegetables to save time for busy people. Although fresh
tends to be best, canned vegetables retain many of their vitamin and mineral
contents. Combining them with ham and a yoghurt-based sauce makes them
more appealing. The beetroot sauce can be substituted for a small amount of
mayonnaise if preferred. The prepared veggies and sauce can be put in containers
and assembled when needed if taken out on a picnic.

Spaghetti à la tomate

Spaghetti in tomato sauce

Serves 6

Ingredients

200g / 7oz spaghetti
1 x 140g / 1 x 5oz tin tomato paste
100ml / 3½fl oz water
1 red capsicum
1 garlic clove
1 courgette
1 tablespoon extra-virgin olive oil
55g / 2oz parmesan

Put the pasta in a saucepan filled with boiling water and cook al dente. Drain well.

Halve and remove the seeds from the capsicum. Cut into small pieces. Peel the garlic. Cut off both ends of the courgette. Chop all the vegetables.

Place in a frying pan with the olive oil. Cook for 10 minutes over medium heat. Mix the tomato paste with the water and add to the vegetables. Mix well. Add the spaghetti and serve with grated parmesan.

You can't go wrong with spaghetti in tomato sauce! This dish is so quick and simple to make but always a success. Add any seasonal vegetable into the mix to increase its nutritional content.

Galettes de pommes de terre et champignons

Mushroom and potato cakes

Makes 8

Ingredients

4 potatoes
3 portabello mushrooms
1 clove garlic
2 tablespoons wholemeal flour
1 egg
2 tablespoons milk
2 tablespoons chopped chives
30g / 1oz cheddar cheese
salt and pepper

Preheat oven to 180°C (350°F). Grease an ovenproof tray or a tray with eight shallow medium-size holes.

Peel and grate the potatoes. Clean and chop the mushrooms. Peel and chop the garlic.

Beat the wholemeal flour with the egg, milk and chives. Mix in the vegetables. Lightly season with salt and pepper.

Shape spoonfuls of this mixture into round flat cakes and place on the prepared tray. Top with grated cheese and bake for 30 minutes. Serve hot or cold.

These mushroom and potato cakes are very versatile and can be served hot or cold, on their own or with some grilled fish or meat, and accompanied with a salad if desired.

Brochettes d'avocat et saumon fumé

Avocado and salmon skewers

Makes 12

Ingredients

- 4 slices smoked salmon
- 12 pitted black olives
- 1 tomato
- 1 avocado
- 12 medium skewers

Halve the avocado, spoon out the flesh and dice into twelve pieces.

Cut each slice of smoked salmon into three pieces.

Cut the tomato into twelve pieces and remove the seeds.

Place one piece of each ingredient onto each skewer and serve as a yummy snack.

The alternate colours and textures of the various ingredients that make up these skewers are interesting to explore for curious little people with budding taste. This snack provides various vitamins and minerals thanks to the fresh vegetables as well as protein and omega 3 fatty acids from the salmon. Cut off both ends of the skewers if preferred to save little fingers from getting pricked.

Tomates farcies

Stuffed tomatoes

Makes 6

Ingredients

 6 tomatoes
 1 shallot
 ½ bunch parsley
 200g / 7oz rump steak
 1 tablespoon extra-virgin olive oil
 1 egg
 30g / 1oz of the inside of a
 wholemeal bread loaf
 55g / 2oz cream cheese
 30g / 1oz gruyere
 salt and pepper

Preheat oven to 180°C (350°F). Grease a large ovenproof dish.

Wash the tomatoes and cut off the opposite side to the stem, setting them aside to use as a lid. Remove the seeds from the tomatoes and sprinkle their flesh with salt. Place upside down on a plate.

Peel and chop the shallot. Wash and finely chop the parsley. Mince the beef and cook over high heat in a frying pan along with the olive oil, shallot and parsley. Remove from the heat and beat in the whole egg, crumbed bread and cream cheese.

Rinse off and dry the tomatoes. Fill them generously with this mixture. Top with some grated gruyere and cover with the reserved tops. Place the tomatoes in the prepared dish and fan bake for 30 minutes. Serve hot.

Wholesome and balanced, this dish can be served to and enjoyed by the whole family. Use tomatoes of various sizes if you wish and serve with a spoon to make it easier for little ones to eat out the filling.

Cannelloni

Lamb and lentil cannelloni

Makes 10

Ingredients

- 1 pack cannelloni
- 1 carrot
- 2 courgettes
- 1 shallot
- 200g / 7oz skinless lamb steak
- ½ x 410g / ½ x 14½oz tin lentils in brine
- 1 tablespoon extra-virgin olive oil
- 1 bay leaf
- 100g / 3½oz cheddar cheese
- 1 x 410g / 1 x 14½oz tin tomatoes in juice

Preheat oven to 180ºC (350ºF). Grease a deep 35 x 27cm (14 x 11 inch) rectangular oven dish.

Peel and grate the carrot. Wash and slice the courgettes. Peel and chop the shallot.

Mince the lamb steak and place in a frying pan along with the prepared vegetables and olive oil. Cook over medium heat for 7-8 minutes or until the meat is cooked through. Add the drained lentils, bay leaf and 100ml / 3½fl oz water.

Cover and cook for a further 10 minutes over low heat. Discard the bay leaf.

Fill each cannelloni with the lamb and vegetable mixture. Place in the prepared dish with any leftover filling. Blend the tomatoes in juice and pour over the cannelloni. Sprinkle with the grated cheddar cheese and fanbake for 35 minutes. Enjoy.

Cannelloni can be filled with virtually any ingredient you fancy. In this recipe I have chosen a mixture of meat, fresh and canned vegetables. Lamb is a good source of B vitamins, iron and zinc and is a meat of choice for growing children. Lentils contain vitamin B6 as well as folate and several minerals such as potassium, iron and manganese.

Preschoolers' Behaviour and Taste

Development

Preschoolers are notorious for being picky eaters. They are at an age where they are getting used to regular mealtimes, and a lot of new tastes and textures, and this can be overwhelming. Refusing food is a way for toddlers to declare their independence and test their parents. They will certainly note your reactions to their refusals or demands with great interest, and will often use these precious pieces of information to their advantage in the future.

To understand why small children eat the way they do, it pays to know about how they develop. Babies grow at a tremendous pace in the first twelve months of their lives. On average, they triple their weight and grow almost 30cm. By the time children turn two, however, their growth rate has slowed to about a tenth of this initial rate. This means that they need proportionally less food than they did when they were babies. Depending on growth spurts, a toddler may need more or less food at different times.

Until about the age of three, children tend to eat according to hunger; older children are more responsive to the quantity of food placed on their plate. This means that the preschool years are an ideal time to encourage children to keep in touch with their inner feelings of hunger and satiety. By serving age-appropriate amounts of food, and listening to what your children tell you, you will avoid distorting their perception of how much food they really need, and this will discourage them from over-eating.

Food intake and portion sizes

One thing is sure: small children don't eat consistently every day. They may love one food for months then suddenly refuse it for no obvious reason. They also have a rather erratic appetite and may just pick at their food for a few days, then eat really well and make up for it during the next few days. This is common, and partly related to growth spurts and their level of activity on a particular day.

Children sometimes eat less in the evening. This may be because they are too tired or simply because they have already had all the food they needed for the day. They may have eaten a large breakfast and a smaller lunch, and sometimes just don't seem interested in dinner at all. Of course this is also dependent on how active they have been during the day, and may vary from day to day. Because their stomach is small, they just don't need that much food to fill it up.

Provided they are offered a large variety of nutritious foods regularly, children will know how much to eat to cover their nutritional needs over a period of a week or so. It is best not to force toddlers to eat, as this overrides their natural ability to regulate their food intake.

When dealing with preschoolers, it is more than likely that you will be placing food on their plate yourself. Serving adult portions would be daunting for your children, not to mention unrealistic and inappropriate. Serve smaller portions and encourage them to ask for seconds. As a rule of thumb, one tablespoon of each type of food per year of age is about right.

Omelette fine

Thin omelette

Serves 4

Ingredients

1 slice ham
1 clove garlic
4 spring onions
6 button mushrooms
1 x 190g / 1 x 6½oz tin bamboo shoots
1 tablespoon extra-virgin olive oil
6 eggs
55ml / 2fl oz milk

Cut the ham into pieces. Peel and chop the garlic. Cut both ends off the spring onions and discard. Finely slice the remaining part. Clean and slice the mushrooms. Drain the bamboo shoots.

Place the ham, spring onions, garlic, mushroom slices and bamboo shoots in a frying pan with the olive oil. Cook over medium heat for 10 minutes.

Beat the eggs and milk together. Pour over the vegetables and cook over high heat until set. Transfer to a plate and cut into slices. Serve warm or cold as a main dish or as a snack.

Omelettes are a great option when there is little time to cook. This dish is a little exotic due to the use of bamboo shoots. Spring onions and mushrooms are very tasty and may be accepted more easily by little children by being mixed with other ingredients. This omelette should be well cooked and cut into strips or slices that can be eaten hot or cold. These make a great finger food and can be served as a healthy snack.

Risotto aux courgettes

Courgette risotto

Serves 4

Ingredients

750ml / 27fl oz water
150g / 5½oz short-grain rice
1 bay leaf
1 tablespoon coriander leaves
½ bunch parsley
1 large courgette
15g / ½oz butter
30g / 1oz parmesan

Bring the water to the boil in a pan and add the rice, bay leaf, coriander leaves and finely chopped parsley. Cook until all of the liquid has been absorbed and the rice is tender. Add some extra water if necessary. Discard the bay leaf.

Wash, cut off both ends of the courgette and finely grate. Mix into the rice along with the butter. Cook for a further 10 minutes over low heat.

Mix in the grated parmesan and cook for another 5 minutes. Leave to stand for a few minutes and serve warm.

I love risotto. Creamy and versatile, risotto suits pretty much every ingredient. I like mixing various vegetables and herbs and often add pieces of meat or fish. This recipe is a vegetarian dish but can be altered with a different choice of seasonal vegetables and the addition of some proteins.

Petits cakes aux carottes

Carrot patties

Makes 24

Ingredients

    5 carrots
    1 purple kumara
    1 clove garlic
    1 egg
    salt and pepper
    ½ broccoli head
    1 teaspoon freshly chopped chives
    2 tablespoons natural yoghurt
    1 teaspoon rubbed parsley

Preheat oven to 180°C (350°F). Grease a mini-muffin tin or use a silicon tin which allows baking without the need to grease.

Peel the carrots, kumara and garlic and cut into pieces. Place in a steamer and cook in the microwave oven on full power for 10 minutes or until tender. Transfer to a mixing bowl and blend into a smooth purée with an electric blender.

Mix in the egg and season lightly with salt and pepper.

To make the broccoli topping, place the broccoli head in a steamer and cook in the microwave oven on full power for five minutes or until tender. Place in a bowl with half the yoghurt and the chives. Blend into a purée with an electric blender.

Place spoonfuls of the carrot mixture into the tin. Use the broccoli mixture as a topping and bake for 20 minutes. Leave to cool before removing from the tin. Serve hot, with the remaining yoghurt mixed with the parsley offered as a dip.

With a puréed texture, these tasty carrot patties will be eaten in no time by your littlies. Use the broccoli topping to make them even more enticing. Carrots are the richest source of beta-carotene while broccoli, with its high levels of fibre, antioxidants, folate and vitamin C, is one of the best vegetables available. You may also want to use the broccoli topping to make smiley faces and letters of the alphabet. My oldest daughter could not resist eating the patties sporting an "N for Noémie".

Pain perdu au fromage

Savoury bread pudding

Serves 4

Ingredients

- 4 slices wholemeal bread
- 4 slices ham
- 15g / ½oz butter
- 3 eggs
- 100ml / 3½fl oz milk
- 1 tablespoon freshly chopped chives
- 55g / 2oz hard tasty cheese such as cheddar or parmesan

Preheat oven to 180°C (350°F). Grease a 20 x 20cm (8 x 8 inch) square ovenproof dish and place the lightly buttered bread slices at the bottom. Top each slice of bread with a slice of ham.

Whisk the eggs with the milk and chives. Pour over the bread and sprinkle with grated cheese. Fan bake in the oven for 20 minutes or until the egg mixture has just set. Serve immediately with a side salad.

This basic dish barely requires any preparation but children just love it. I have used wholemeal bread to increase the fibre content. The ham and eggs provide proteins while the milk and cheese help meet a child's daily calcium requirements.

Boulettes de tofu et lentilles

Tofu and lentil balls

Makes 15

Ingredients

1 small shallot
1 clove garlic
300g / 10½oz cooked lentils
240g / 8½oz tofu
1 tablespoon extra-virgin olive oil
2 egg yolks
55g / 2oz wholemeal flour

Guacamole yoghurt dip
½ avocado
1 teaspoon lemon juice
3 tablespoons Greek-style yoghurt
1 teaspoon avocado oil
salt and pepper

Preheat oven to 180°C (350°F). Grease an ovenproof tray.

Peel and slice the shallot and garlic. Place in a food processor with the lentils, crumbed tofu and the olive oil. Process until well blended. Mix in the egg yolks and fold in the flour.

Using your fingers, shape spoonfuls of this mixture into small balls and place on the prepared tray until all the mixture has been used up. Fan bake in the oven for 30 minutes.

To make the guacamole yoghurt dip, purée the flesh of the avocado with a fork. Drizzle with lemon juice and add the yoghurt and avocado oil. Season with salt and pepper and mix until well combined. Serve with the tofu and lentil balls.

This original recipe was a hit at home. Children love the concept of finger food and always enjoy a homemade dip – it increases the fun factor of any meal. Vegetarian people will appreciate the use of tofu. Tofu has the health benefits of soy beans, which are among the few plant sources of complete protein and which can help lower LDL blood cholesterol among other things. The Guacamole yoghurt dip can also be used to accompany sticks of raw vegetables.

Terrine de légumes

Vegetable terrine

Serves 8

Ingredients

½ x 340g / ½ x 12oz tin peas
¼ x 340g / ¼ x 12oz tin green beans
¼ x 340g / ¼ x 12oz tin baby carrots
½ x 340g / ½ x 12oz tin corn kernels
½ x 210g / ½ x 7½oz tin salmon in brine
6 eggs
150ml / 5fl oz milk

Preheat oven to 180°C (350°F). Grease a 23 x 12cm (9 x 5 inch) loaf tin.

Drain all the vegetables, place in a bowl and mix well. Crumb the salmon, making sure to discard any bone, and add to the vegetables. Place at the bottom of the prepared tin.

Whisk the eggs with the milk. Pour over the vegetables.

Fan bake for 30 minutes or until just set, cut into slices and serve warm or cold.

This is yet another very simple, quick recipe which can be a life-saver on a busy week night. Making use of tinned vegetables that are pantry basics as well as eggs, salmon and milk, it provides virtually everything your children need in just one dish. It may be eaten warm or cold and accompanied with some tomato sauce. This terrine makes a great picnic lunch item.

Preschoolers' Behaviour and Taste - continued

Introducing new foods

Research has shown that familiarity is a primary factor when it comes to children's behaviour towards food. Littlies thrive on routine, and may be afraid of new experiences in the same way they can be afraid of new people. They enjoy eating familiar foods. Your goal as a parent is to increase the number of foods that your children are familiar with. This will ensure that they get an appropriate nutrient intake and help them develop healthy eating habits.

Do not be put off by a few refusals when you offer new foods. Studies have shown that you may have to offer a new food to a toddler ten or more times before he eventually tries it (but it is comforting to know that he will eventually!). The more effort you put into presenting a new food in an appealing way, the more likely you are to succeed. You may also like to offer a small sample of the new food before mealtime, maybe as a snack. If your child is adamant about not trying the food, wait for a few days and try introducing the food again until eventually they accept it. However, you should acknowledge and respect the fact that small children have some food dislikes, just like adults do. If they really don't like a food, look for appropriate substitutes. No one food is essential; only food groups are.

If your child is tired or upset, this is just not the right time to introduce a new food. It may even cause your child to refuse that same food on later occasions. Be patient and seize the opportunities as they arise, but don't force them.

Tips

Children naturally have a sweet tooth. Their first food, usually breast milk, is very sweet indeed. Toddlers learn to enjoy savoury foods, but they need to be offered these foods often. Even though they love putting everything into their mouths – especially things you wish never got there – they tend to be wary and can show significant resistance when it comes to new foods. This means that parents have to be patient and realistic in their expectations. By all means, offer new, healthy foods on a regular basis but don't be too eager. Diversify your children's diet slowly. Snack time may be a good time to offer new foods, as some children refuse food at mealtimes but accept them at snack time. Make healthful snacks readily available and you may be surprised at your children's responses.

It may pay to sneak new foods into a favourite meal to start with. Grate a less favourite vegetable, or add some minced meat or crumbed fish, into a dish you know they love. They will hardly notice it and once they are well into eating the "sneaky dish" you can point out the pieces of new food they are enjoying. Show them the raw vegetable or other ingredient so they can find it in the shop later on. Doing this will create a positive association and they are more likely to accept a meal with the same food (unhidden!) later.

Galettes de potimarron

Pumpkin cakes

Makes 6

Ingredients

½ grey pumpkin (approximately 300g / 10½oz pumpkin flesh)
1 kumara
125g / 4½oz chicken
1 tablespoon extra-virgin olive oil
½ bunch parsley
1 egg
55g / 2oz cheddar cheese
salt and pepper

Vegetable baskets

6 tomatoes
10cm / 4in cucumber
6 radishes
12 pitted black olives

To make the vegetable baskets, place the tomatoes on a plate, stem down. Make a horizontal cut close to the top but stop before getting to the middle. Make a similar horizontal cut on the other side. On each side, make a vertical cut to take out two pieces of tomato and make a handle.

Remove all the seeds from the tomatoes. Cut the pieces of tomatoes that were taken out into small pieces. Peel and cut the cucumber into small pieces. Slice the olives and the radishes. Mix these vegetables together and use to fill the tomato baskets.

Prepare the pumpkin cakes. Preheat oven to 180°C (350°F). Remove the flesh from the pumpkin and peel the kumara. Cut into chunks. Place in a steamer and cook in the microwave on full power for eight minutes.

Mince the chicken in a food processor. Place in a frying pan and cook thoroughly with the olive oil. Wash and dry the parsley. Process the pumpkin, kumara and parsley into a smooth purée with an electrical blender. Mix in the cooked chicken, the whole egg and half the grated cheese. Divide this mixture between six silicon tartlet tins and sprinkle with the remaining cheese. Fan bake for 25 minutes or until golden and serve warm with the vegetable baskets.

These yummy pumpkin cakes are choc-a-block with nutrients. Parsley has numerous virtues including a high content of vitamin C while pumpkin is full of carotene. The chicken and egg add some proteins while hard cheese such as cheddar provides a high level of calcium.

Fresh Start

Rouleaux d'épinards

Makes 12

Ingredients

    2 carrots
    1 bunch spinach
    2 tablespoons extra-virgin olive oil
    240g / 8½oz white fish such as red cod or gurnard
    55g / 2oz feta cheese
    1 egg
    1 egg yolk
    1 tablespoon milk
    8 sheets filo pastry
    24 straws of fresh chives

If using frozen filo pastry, remove from the freezer and thaw in the fridge for a couple of hours.

Preheat oven to 180°C (350°F). Grease a large ovenproof tray. Peel and grate the carrots. Wash and drain the spinach. Place in a wok with half the olive oil and a couple of tablespoons water. Cook over medium heat for about 10 minutes.

Remove from the wok and set aside. Place the fish with the remaining oil in the wok and cook over high heat until thoroughly cooked. Place on a plate and crumb, making sure to discard any bone.

Mix the crumbed fish with the cooked vegetables. Add the diced feta cheese. Beat in one whole egg.

Stack two sheets of filo pastry on a flat surface and cut into three pieces along the smallest side. Place a spoonful of the fish mixture at the smallest end of each piece of filo pastry and roll up. Use two straws of fresh chive to secure each end of the fish and spinach wrap and place on the prepared tray. Repeat until all the filo pastry sheets and filling have been used up.

Mix the egg yolk with the milk and use to lightly spread over the top of the filo wraps. Bake for 30 minutes or until golden and crispy. Serve with a side salad.

I like wraps – they are so like presents. Whatever is inside is a surprise and tasting is always exciting. Wrapping veggies and fish can be a good idea if your children are particularly picky. They may be less resistant to food presented in this manner.

Flans d'asperges

Asparagus flans

Makes 5

Ingredients

> 240g / 8½oz fresh asparagus
> 2 eggs
> 30g / 1oz feta cheese
> 55g / 2oz Greek-style yoghurt
> salt and pepper

Preheat oven to 180°C (350°F). Grease five individual baking tins.

Drain the asparagus and place in a mixing bowl with the eggs, feta cheese and Greek-style yoghurt. Process into a smooth purée with an electric blender. Season with salt and pepper.

Pour this mixture into the prepared tins and fan bake for 25 minutes or until just set. Serve warm or cold.

These little flans are suitable for all children. Asparagus have many virtues, including that of being one of the few good vegetable sources of vitamin E. They are also a natural diuretic. Mixed with eggs and cheese, they make a yummy and nutritious lunch for little people. When not in season, make this dish with tinned asparagus.

Purée de poulet

Chicken purée

Serves 2 to 4

Ingredients

>80g / 3oz skinless chicken breast
>2 small courgettes
>½ banana
>1 teaspoon fresh parsley
>1 tablespoon natural yoghurt
>salt and pepper

Wash and chop the parsley. Mince the chicken and place in a frying pan with the parsley. Cook with the olive oil for 10 minutes over high heat or until cooked through.

Slice the courgettes and the banana and add to the pan. Cook for a further 10 minutes.

Transfer the chicken and courgettes into a mixing bowl. Add the yoghurt and season with salt and pepper. Process into a smooth purée.

Divide between two to four bowls depending on the children's ages and appetite. Serve warm.

This recipe suits babies just starting on solid foods. The ingredients are blended together for a smooth, puréed consistency and combine savoury and sweet. The quantities can be increased and any extra mixture can be frozen into ice-cube blocks for later use.

Managing Mealtimes

Making meals pleasant

It is when your children are the youngest that you have the most control over them. Once they start school and eat out regularly, their friends and convenience shops will have a lot of influence on them. So use the preschool years to instil in them a love for nutritious foods and the satisfaction of eating a balanced diet, and to teach them good table manners.

Making meals a pleasant experience is important. After all, they take place three times a day in most cases. There are a few things you can do to look forward to mealtimes instead of dreading the moment. Mealtimes are an opportunity for small children to show their independence – and they often do so! They may turn down the food you have put on their plates and refuse to sit down for long. There are many techniques and punishments that work reasonably well to get children to do as they are told, but it is even better if they willingly do what you want them to do.

Tips

Children need to feel comfortable and unpressured to be able to enjoy eating. They will love being involved in a conversation, but try not to focus too much on the food itself. Talk about their day, and yours, instead.

Let your preschoolers feed themselves as much as possible. By age two, most children can sit at a table and hold their own spoon or fork. Finger food is also empowering for small children, as it makes it easier for them to feed themselves and choose what to eat out of the variety of foods offered. It is a good way to introduce new foods and textures.

Meals can be a messy affair, but if you give the children unbreakable tableware and cups that have a handle, or can be held with both hands, it will be safer and easier for them and you may be able to do some damage control. If the prospect of having to mop the floor after each meal does not appeal to you, place a large plastic sheet under and around your children's chairs. After the meal you can just shake the plastic sheet outside and then put it away.

Be open about letting children combine foods that don't traditionally mix and match. After all, if your children would like to have some banana with their meat or dip a carrot in berry sauce, what harm can it do? What matters is that they learn to eat healthy foods. If making rather weird mixtures can help them do so, don't let it bother you!

Remember that children learn by watching you and imitating you rather than through criticism or lectures (in fact, this may even cause resentment and antagonism). I am not suggesting that you should give in to your children's every whim. But try to simply appear uninterested when things don't go the way you want during a meal. Continue setting the example you want your children to model themselves on.

Try to be firm and not to give in when your children ask for alternatives to the meal you have prepared for them. And be consistent. If they have refused to eat one meal, and know when the next snack or meal will be coming, do not let them snack until that time. Do not give snacks just before a meal as a pacifier or a way to pass the time. Having a small snack an hour or two before a meal is fine, but anything closer and your children are less likely to be hungry for the actual meal (not to mention they will get used to eating constantly and at no particular time).

Refuse to engage in a food fight or power struggle over food. Don't worry if your children occasionally leave their meal half-eaten. They may genuinely not be hungry or feel unwell. At the end of the day, they know if their tummies are full and will let you know if they need more food. Making a big issue of the situation is just going to make things worse, as your children are likely to become even more determined not to eat their meal. Always try not to make food the object of bribes or punishment.

Finally be relaxed! This is not always easy to say the least but the atmosphere in which you offer food is important. If you get all stressed out just trying to get your children to come and sit down for a meal, you are unlikely to get the results you are after. Try to remain relaxed (or at least to appear relaxed!) and avoid making a fuss even when they are being difficult or not eating at all. The more you insist the more they refuse. Bear in mind that although a toddler's eating can be unpredictable, viewed over several days he will meet his average needs provided he is offered an appropriate variety of different foods. So don't sweat the small stuff and be assured that any missed meal will be made up for elsewhere.

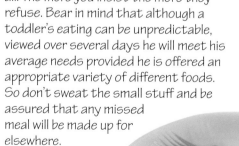

Rouleaux de jambon

Ham rolls

Makes 12

Ingredients

12 toothpicks
4 slices ham
55g / 2oz cream cheese
1 tablespoon coriander leaves
½ tomato

Place a slice of ham on a plate and spread with a small amount of cream cheese. Use a knife to cut into three strips and roll up.

Secure with a toothpick and repeat until all the ham and cheese have been used up. Sprinkle with the finely chopped coriander leaves and serve with a few bite-sized and pip-free pieces of tomato.

These snacks take just a few minutes to make and provide both protein and calcium. They are also easy for little children to munch on. Even very young children can help you make them, for example spreading the cream cheese or rolling up the ham. Make sure to cut off both ends of the toothpicks after securing the rolls to save your littlies from pricking their fingers.

Crêpes au jambon et au fromage

Ham and cheese pancakes

Makes 4

Ingredients

Wholemeal pancake batter
70g / 2½oz wholemeal flour
70g / 2½oz rye flour
1 egg
55ml / 2fl oz water
250ml / 9fl oz milk
½ teaspoon salt
1 tablespoon vegetable oil
Filling
4 slices ham
70g / 2½oz grated cheese
30g / 1oz butter

To make the wholemeal pancake batter, place the wholemeal flour and the rye flour in a bowl. Mix in the egg and water to obtain a smooth paste. Gradually blend in the milk. Add the salt and vegetable oil. Leave at room temperature for an hour before use.

Heat a large frying pan and add a small amount of butter. Pour half a cup of the pancake batter and cook over high heat until just set. Turn over and cook for a further 30 seconds. Transfer to a large plate. Repeat until all the batter has been used up.

To garnish, place a pancake in the frying pan. Top with a slice of ham and some grated cheese. Cook over medium heat for a few minutes to allow the cheese to melt. Roll and serve immediately with a few shredded lettuce leaves.

This specialty from Brittany is very versatile and there are as many fillings as you can dream up. When I was a child we enjoyed the ham and cheese pancakes that my mum made for us very much. They are a hit with most children. The unfilled pancakes will keep for a couple of days in an airtight container placed in the fridge and can be filled and reheated just before serving.

Gratinée de poisson

Serves 4

Ingredients

3 potatoes
300g / 10½oz fresh green beans
½ bunch parsley
450g / 1lb red cod
1 tablespoon extra-virgin olive oil
2 hard-boiled eggs
150g / 5½oz condensed mushroom soup
150ml / 5fl oz milk
55g / 2oz cheddar cheese
1 tablespoon dill
1 lemon
2 tablespoons breadcrumbs

Preheat oven to 180°C (350°F). Grease a deep ovenproof dish. Peel the potatoes and cook for 15 minutes in a steamer. Cut both ends off the beans and cook for 10 minutes in a steamer. Wash and finely chop the parsley.

Cook the fish in a frying pan with the olive oil, lemon juice and dill. Set aside on a plate, crumb and make sure to discard any bone. Shell and slice the eggs. Slice the potatoes.

Place the sliced potatoes in the prepared dish. Cover with the crumbed fish and half the chopped parsley. Top with the green beans and slices of hard-boiled eggs.

Mix the condensed soup with the milk and use to cover the fish and vegetables. Sprinkle with the grated cheese, remaining parsley and breadcrumbs. Fan bake for 30 minutes. Serve hot.

This is another great way to serve fish to resistant children. They are more likely to accept it when it is mixed with a variety of other favourite ingredients such as eggs, cheese and potatoes. This dish makes a warming and hearty dinner and will be particularly appreciated on a cool day. The mushroom soup may be substituted for another flavour of your choice. Out of season, use tinned green beans instead of fresh ones, or another seasonal vegetable.

Purée de carottes au jambon

Carrot and ham purée

Serves 4

Ingredients

6 carrots
1 potato
1 onion
1 clove garlic
½ bunch parsley
30g / 1oz butter
100ml / 3½fl oz milk
4 slices ham
salt and pepper

Peel the vegetables. Cut the carrots and potato into chunks, slice the onion and chop the garlic. Wash and dry the parsley. Place all these ingredients in a steamer and cook over high heat until tender.

Transfer to a mixing bowl and process into a smooth purée with an electric blender. Add the butter and stir until melted. Gradually mix in the milk to obtain the desired consistency. Lightly season with salt and pepper.

Divide between four bowls and top with finely chopped ham. Serve warm.

My mum made this purée several times while on a visit to New Zealand with my dad. Each time, the children asked for more and there was never any leftover. It is a fairly basic but tasty recipe – and it was such a success. It has become known as "Nana's purée" and is requested on a regular basis.

Velouté de courgettes

Cream of courgette soup

Serves 4

Ingredients

4 courgettes
80g / 3oz plain cream cheese
1 shallot
1 tablespoon freshly chopped parsley
250ml / 9fl oz water
salt and pepper

Cut off both ends of the courgettes and slice. Peel and chop the shallot. Cook in a steamer for a few minutes until tender.

Place in a food processor with the cream cheese and blend into a smooth purée. Gradually mix in the water to obtain a runny texture. Add the parsley. Heat up and serve warm with a slice of bread.

This recipe requires very little time and ingredients but the result is tasty and suitable for children of any age. You may wish to use half water, half milk instead of just water. This will increase the creaminess of this soup as well as its calcium contents.

Méli-mélo aux épinards

Spinach medley

Serves 4

Ingredients

- 4 eggs
- 330ml / 12fl oz unsweetened condensed milk
- 1 bunch spinach
- 100g / 3½oz ricotta cheese
- 1 tablespoon extra-virgin olive oil
- 1 teaspoon dried mixed herbs

Preheat oven to 180°C (350°F). Grease a 20 x 20cm (8 x 8 inch) square tin.

Wash and drain the spinach. Place in a frying pan with the olive oil and mixed herbs. Cover and cook over medium heat for a few minutes. Mix in the crumbed ricotta cheese.

Whisk the eggs with the condensed milk. Beat the egg mixture with the cooked spinach and pour into the prepared tin. Fan bake for 20 minutes or until just set. Serve warm.

Some vegetables can be difficult to make look exciting, and many will agree that spinach may well be one of them. However mix it with various herbs and it will instantly become tastier; add some cheese and condensed milk to add creaminess and throw in a few eggs and you are onto a winner. The green stuff will be seen under a new light! And more importantly, your children will actually agree to eat it.

Making Food Fun

A sure way to increase interest in fruit, vegetables, meat, fish, and other foods full of positive nutritional value is to increase the fun factor. This involves spending a little extra time styling the food specifically to appeal to young children. Children love food that is served in a fun and clever way, and they are more likely to try new foods and foods that they normally wouldn't eat. Appropriate presentation truly makes a difference.

Be creative! You don't need a cooking degree for this. Use your imagination to make what may be not-so-interesting food appear more interesting to toddlers. Try some simple but creative ideas to turn everyday meals into something special. This will entice your children to eat the foods you want them to eat. For example:

- Fill up empty squeeze bottles with various sauces – homemade or bought, savoury and sweet. Let them squeeze some onto their meal themselves.

- Use the sauces to write your children's names, make smiley (or sad) faces, and draw pictures such as people, houses, the moon, the stars, and the sun on their plates. Fill the centre of each shape with fruit or vegetables pieces if you want to.

- Shape food to look like their favourite animal, using condiments or pieces of raw vegetable to make the eyes, mouth, ears, nose, and tail.

- Use cookie cutters of various shapes and sizes to make sandwiches, or to make slices of fruit, cheese, or ham more interesting.

- Use vegetable sticks to make numbers and write your child's age.

Be warned that the results may not always be what you expect. It can be depressing to make the extra effort only to have your children push away their plates and declare that they will not have any of the food lovingly prepared for them. But it often works well, and in the long run it is worth persisting and consistently offering food in a way that has some sort of excitement factor.

More mealtimes tips

Offer a piece of fruit or a few veggie sticks first thing rather than waiting for your children to fill up on other foods. At least you know they will get some vitamins and minerals in their meal. Also give them proteins when they are most hungry and serve fatty and sugary foods last and in small portions.

Always offer a wide array of different foods, especially colourful food. By buying seasonal foods, you will avoid blowing your budget, and you will encourage your kids to try out new foods and be more in tune with what nature has to offer. For example, place a selection of whole baby vegetables, vegetable sticks, and florets in a bowl, along with a dip, for your kids to pick from. Preparing an attractive platter full of nutritious easy-to-eat foods such as veggie sticks, homemade dips, quartered hard-boiled eggs and cheese cubes is likely to make your children interested and willing to try many of the foods on offer.

Give special consideration to textures, like foods that crunch under the bite or that melt on the tongue. A change in texture can instantly make the same food look a lot more appealing to a young child. Add interest to food by inventing stories where carrots stand for magic sticks, orange slices for smiles, and so on. Play games comparing sizes, colours, and shapes, or finding foods that start with each letter of the alphabet.

Occasionally offer the option of eating in a different place. No meal has ever had more success than when I took our picnic rug out

and set out my children's meal on the lawn, complete with paper plates, paper cups, and serviettes. The added bonus is the absence of mess to clean up afterwards (well, except for the grass-stained clothes). The playhouse outdoors, a makeshift marquee indoors (made by attaching a sheet to a few pieces of furniture), and a tea party setup have worked well too.

Gratin de pommes de terre et brocolis

Potato and broccoli gratin

Serves 4

Ingredients

150g / 5½oz chicken breast
1 tablespoon extra-virgin olive oil
3 potatoes
2 broccoli heads
100g / 3½oz feta cheese
200ml / 7fl oz milk
8 eggs
30g / 1oz cheddar cheese

Preheat oven to 180°C (350°F). Grease a 20 x 20cm (8 x 8 inch) square tin.

Cut the chicken into strips and cook in a frying pan with the olive oil.

Peel and slice the potatoes. Cut the spears off the broccoli heads and chop into small pieces. Place the vegetables at the bottom of the prepared dish. Top with the cooked chicken and diced feta cheese.

Whisk the eggs with the milk. Pour this mixture over the vegetables and sprinkle with grated cheddar cheese. Fan bake for 35 minutes or until golden. Serve warm with a few slices of tomato or shredded lettuce leaves.

Broccoli is without doubt one of the best vegetable around. It is high in fibre, beta-carotene, vitamin C and folate. It is also thought to protect from some forms of cancer. I try to use it often, as it is available most of the year. In addition to having some health benefits it is tasty too. Gratins are often favoured by children so baking food this way is a good opportunity to introduce new foods. I have substituted the traditional cheese sauce for an egg and milk mixture which is lighter but just as nutritious.

Bâtons aux carottes et au tofu

Tofu and carrot fingers

Makes 8

Ingredients

1 leek
360g / 12½oz grated carrots
240g / 8½oz tofu
2 eggs
1 tablespoon light soy sauce
2 tablespoons sesame seeds
2 tablespoons breadcrumbs
1 tablespoon extra-virgin olive oil

Preheat oven to 180°C (350°F). Grease a 23 x 12cm (9 x 5 inch) loaf tin.

Wash the leek and finely chop the white base and the pale end of the stalks. Place in a frying pan along with the grated carrots and olive oil. Cook over medium heat for 10 minutes or until tender.

Remove from the pan and place in a mixing bowl. Beat in the crumbed tofu, whole eggs, soy sauce and sesame seeds.

Pour this mixture into the prepared tin, sprinkle with breadcrumbs and fan bake for 25 minutes. Leave to cool. Cut into slices and serve.

Here is a different way to serve carrots. In this recipe they are complemented with tofu, a vegetarian ingredient of choice and also a good alternative to dairy products. The fingers have a soft texture and are best eaten with a spoon.

Barquettes de concombre

Cucumber boaties

Makes 12

Ingredients

   1 cucumber
   2 hard-boiled eggs
   125g / 4½oz cottage cheese
   1 tomato
   1 tablespoon fresh chives

Peel and halve the cucumber. Remove the pips and cut each half into six segments. Peel the tomato and remove the pips. Cut the flesh into small pieces.

Shell and crumble the hard-boiled eggs and mix with the cottage cheese. Add the pieces of tomato to the egg mixture.

Use this mixture to fill the cucumber segments. Sprinkle with the finely chopped chives. Serve chilled as a healthy snack or on a picnic.

What a cute way to serve cucumber! Crunchy and refreshing, it makes a great summer vegetable. Cottage cheese and eggs complement it nicely and transform it into a nutritious snack.

Chaussons au thon

Makes 4

Ingredients

12 sheets filo pastry
2 Portobello mushrooms
1 shallot
2 tablespoons fresh chives
1 x 185g / 1 x 6½oz tin tuna in brine
1 egg
½ lemon, juiced
55g / 2oz feta cheese
1 egg yolk
1 tablespoon milk

Preheat oven to 180ºC (350ºF). Grease an ovenproof tray.

Clean and chop the mushrooms. Peel and chop the shallot. Finely chop the chives. Drain the tuna and beat with one whole egg and the lemon juice. Mix in the chopped mushrooms, shallot and chives. Add the crumbed feta cheese.

Stack three sheets of filo pastry on a flat surface. Place a quarter of the tuna filling in the centre of the pastry and fold to close the tuna pocket. Repeat until the filo pastry and tuna mixture have been used up.

Place the tuna pockets on the prepared tray. Mix the egg yolk with the milk and use to lightly brush the top of the tuna pockets. Fan bake for 30 minutes or until golden.

These pockets can be made with any fish or meat of your choice. The recipe would suit salmon as well as chicken very well if you are ever looking at varying the taste. Again, presenting new ingredients and vegetables in this manner makes it more likely for children to try them.

Pâtes aux champignons

Mushroom pasta

Serves 4

Ingredients

125g / 4½oz pasta
150g / 5½oz button mushrooms
100g / 3½oz ham
1 tablespoon extra-virgin olive oil
½ broccoli head
30g / 1oz parmesan
100ml / 3½fl oz unsweetened
condensed milk
salt and pepper

Put the pasta in a saucepan filled with boiling water and cook al dente. Drain well.

Clean and slice the mushrooms. Cut the ham into small pieces. Place in a frying pan along with the mushrooms and olive oil. Cook over medium heat until crispy.

Cut the spears off the broccoli heads and chop into small pieces. Add to the pan and cook for another five minutes. Mix in the condensed milk, pasta and grated cheese. Lightly season with salt and pepper. Stir for a few more minutes over low heat until the cheese has melted.

Pasta is a traditional children's favourite and there are countless ways to serve them. Try something different this time and mix in some mushrooms and broccoli. Parmesan is very strong and gives a great flavour to any pasta dish without the need to use lots of it.

Carrots are high in beta-carotene and antioxidants. They can be served in many ways, whether as raw sticks, grated, puréed or sliced. Young children may prefer them finely sliced and cooked as they will be softer to chew.

Semoule aux carottes

Carrots with cous cous

Serves 4

Ingredients

4 carrots
1 tablespoon extra-virgin olive oil
1 teaspoon dried mixed herbs
100ml / 3½fl oz water
55g / 2oz feta cheese
100g / 3½oz cous cous
15g / ½oz butter
salt and pepper

Peel and slice the carrots. Place in a frying pan with the olive oil and mixed herbs. Add the water and cover. Cook over medium heat for 15 minutes or until tender. Uncover and cook for another five minutes over high heat. Remove from the heat and mix in the crumbed feta cheese. Lightly season with salt and pepper.

Pour the cous cous into a bowl and cover with just enough boiling water to reach 1cm / ½ inch over the cous cous. Cover and leave for a few minutes until all the water has been absorbed.

Using a fork, separate the cous cous grains. Mix in the butter until melted. Cook in a microwave oven for a few minutes and serve with the carrots.

Sweet treats

Sweets and Treats

Making sweets part of a balanced diet

It is unrealistic to try to eliminate all fatty and sugary foods from children's diets. In fact, totally banning treats from your child's diet is unlikely to have the desired result. The more restrictive the sugar policy, the more fixated on eating forbidden foods children become. The last thing you want is for an over-strict eating regime to cause an eating disorder.

Treats can be part of a healthy diet. They just need to be considered as such, and to only be offered infrequently or on special occasions. Take a reasonable approach and integrate such foods in appropriate quantities as part of your children's healthy diet.

It is a good idea to make desserts that contain a good nutritional value. That way, even if your children refuse to eat the first part of their meal properly, you will not feel bad about giving them dessert. Even better, dessert will provide them with some important nutrients that they would not have otherwise eaten. Try a fruity rice pudding (see recipe on page 86), fresh fruit salads and cooked dried fruit salads (see recipes on pages 75 and 82), plain yoghurt mixed with fruit and spices (try recipes on pages 93 and 99) and cakes made with wholemeal flour and full of dried or fresh fruit (see recipes on pages 70 and 106).

You can also lessen the temptation by not over-emphasising dessert and not making it a habitual daily event. The last thing you are aiming for is to attach emotional baggage to food or for children to hold out on eating the nutritious main meal with the expectation that they will get dessert. Using sweets as a reward or bribe for eating veggies is not a good idea. Try not to use sweets to calm a meltdown, as it may also encourage an unhealthy association between eating certain foods and emotional comfort.

To keep in mind

It may seem surprising but introducing sweets to your children yourself may be the best option. Otherwise they will get their own ideas from friends or the television. This may not be the best thing. When you do offer sweets, just make sure to keep portions small. Sugar is not that bad at all, as long as it is consumed in moderation.

For dental health, what matters most is the amount of time that the food remains in the mouth, rather than the food itself. An important rule with sweets is to insist that your children brush their teeth after eating anything sticky, crumbly, or sugary. This will help keep tooth damage under control. Whenever possible, have your children brush their teeth right after they have finished eating.

Cake aux fruits confits

Fruit loaf

Serves 8

Ingredients

- 125g / 4½oz unsalted butter
- 55g / 2oz icing sugar
- 3 tablespoons honey
- 3 eggs
- 125g / 4½oz white flour
- 70g / 2½oz rye flour
- 1 teaspoon baking powder
- 55ml / 2fl oz milk
- 40g / 1½oz red glacé cherries
- 40g / 1½oz green glacé cherries
- 55g / 2oz sultanas

Preheat oven to 160°C (325°F). Grease a 23 × 12cm (9 × 5 inch) loaf tin. Melt the butter and mix in the icing sugar and honey. Beat in the eggs and mix until well combined.

Fold in the white flour, rye flour and baking powder. Add the milk and mix well. Mix in the glacé cherries and sultanas.

Pour this batter into the prepared tin and fan bake for 35 minutes or until a fine skewer or toothpick inserted into the centre of the cake comes out clean. Slice up and serve warm or cold.

This fruit loaf is delicious and naturally sweet thanks to the fruit. It only needs the addition of a small amount of sugar and honey. For children under the age of one, substitute the honey with sugar or omit altogether. Using rye flour has the added benefit of providing some extra fibre into your children's diet. Serve this loaf warm or cold with a glass of milk as a nutritious and healthy snack.

Iles aux fruits rouges

Berry islands

Serves 4

Ingredients

- 1 x 410g / 1 x 14½oz tin mixed berries in syrup
- 2 egg whites
- pinch of salt
- 30g / 1oz sugar
- 1 teaspoon vanilla essence
- 15g / ½oz dark chocolate

Drain the berries and set aside two tablespoons of the syrup. Place the berries in a food processor and process into a smooth purée. Add the reserved syrup to obtain a runny texture.

Whip the egg whites with a pinch of salt until firm. Mix in the sugar and vanilla essence.

Bring some water to the boil in a saucepan. Place spoonfuls of egg whites in the boiling water and cook for 30 seconds on each side. Remove from the water and drain. Repeat until all the egg whites have been cooked.

Divide the berry sauce between four dessert bowls and top with the egg white islands. Put the chocolate into a small cup with one tablespoon water and cook in the microwave for a few seconds. Stir to melt the chocolate and obtain a smooth texture. Use to top the islands.

Light, colourful and airy, this dessert is fun and delicious. The egg whites provide proteins while the use of tinned berries makes it an all-year-round dessert. Of course, in season you could certainly use luscious, fresh berries in their place.

Coupelles de chocolat au yaourt

Chocolate yoghurt cups

Makes 10

Ingredients

100g / 3½oz dark chocolate
100g / 3½oz Greek-style yoghurt
30g / 1oz sugar
1 teaspoon vanilla bean paste

Break the chocolate into pieces and melt in a bowl set over a pan of gently simmering water. Pour a thin layer of melted chocolate into ten small paper cases. Chill for 15 minutes or until set.

Mix the yoghurt with the sugar and vanilla bean paste. Spoon a little of this mixture into each chocolate cup. Chill and decorate with hundreds and thousands before serving if desired.

This recipe is indulgent yet actually quite healthy. Each cup contains little dark chocolate, which is good in small amounts as among other things, it happens to be a source of iron and magnesium. The filling has a delicious vanilla flavour and contains the goodness of yoghurt. These cups make an ideal guilt-free children's party food. I just love the natural vanilla taste of the vanilla bean paste that I buy from the supermarket. Having said that, it may be substituted for natural vanilla essence if preferred.

Salade de fruits

Fruit salad

Serves 4 to 6

Ingredients

2 apples
2 pears
2 kiwi fruits
1 pink grapefruit
1 banana
½ lemon, juiced
1 tablespoon honey
1 teaspoon vanilla essence

Peel the apples and pears and cut into small chunks. Peel and slice the kiwi fruits and the banana. Halve and remove the flesh from the grapefruit. Place the fruit into a bowl.

Squeeze the grapefruit halves to remove any juice and pour over the fruit, along with the lemon juice and vanilla essence. Drizzle the honey on top and mix well. Divide between four to six cups and serve immediately.

A fruit salad is fresh and simple. Its success depends on the quality and sweetness of the fruit used. For children under the age of one, substitute the honey with sugar or omit altogether. Make sure to use seasonal ripe fruit and cut them into small enough pieces. Serve as a healthy dessert alternative or as a vitamin-packed snack.

Getting Children Involved

Learning about food

The more you involve your children in the process of preparing and cooking food, the more likely it is that they will become healthy eaters. Involving children in food shopping and food preparation is sure to pay off. It catches their attention and gets them interested in new foods and tastes, which in turn will gently direct them towards eating a varied, balance diet for life. Fruit and vegetables suddenly become a lot more exciting if your children have been helping out planting, looking after, and harvesting a small garden. This can be done even if your backyard is on the small side. If you live in an apartment, you can plant radishes, strawberries, parsley, dill, mint, and other herbs in small pots.

If a veggie garden is not your thing, or you just don't have time for one, find out where your nearest pick-your-own farm is located and make picking your own strawberries, raspberries, or blueberries a fun family activity. When you get home, turn the berries into homemade jams, tarts, fruit salads, sorbets, and fruit yoghurt. Even involving your children in shopping for fruit and veggies can be helpful, if you shop for these at a specialist shop and don't have to go through the biscuit, chips, and chocolate aisles at the supermarket.

While shopping or looking after your garden, seize the opportunity and take

the time to explain to your children what each fruit and vegetable can be used for. Preschoolers are thirsty for knowledge and will love learning about the season when each product will be ready for harvest, what colour it should be when ripe, whether it contains a stone or pips, whether or not it needs to be peeled or cooked, whether it is sour, acid, or sweet, and so on.

Cooking together

Another way to make a child interested in eating nutritious foods is to involve them in the preparation. If my kids are anything to go by, getting children interested in ice-creams or chocolate cookies is not a challenge at all, but vegetables can be a different story. A child's level of involvement will vary depending on his age, but even very young children can help in some way. Always keep safety in mind and do not involve small children in cutting meat or veggies with a sharp knife, or in handling hot dishes.

Explain to your children what type of dish or dessert you are making. Ask them what they think of adding this or that ingredient, what difference they think it will make to the taste, and how much of the ingredient they think you should have, and they will love it even more. You can gently direct their answers, but always make them feel like their input and their help is extremely important to you.

When I cook, I often set out ingredients on the small children's table where the girls can help me easily, and put my youngest one in the highchair where he can watch us. Although I do the peeling and chopping myself, I always let the girls mix and throw in some ingredients (who cares if we end up with a little too much dill or an overly generous dose of vanilla essence!), pour the batter for a cake into the tin (with a little help), sprinkle sliced almonds on top of a dessert to decorate, or garnish the plates with a few sprigs of fresh parsley or dill from our veggie garden before serving. Even babies as young as one will enjoy helping, and just seeing how proud it makes them is worth the few minutes longer that it takes to have involved the children. Doing such things will entice them to try and taste the new ingredients you are using for a particular recipe. This is how one of my daughters had her first taste of raw garlic!

Gâteau aux carottes

Carrot torte

Serves 12

Ingredients

150g / 5½oz ground almonds
150g / 5½oz whole hazelnuts
1 tablespoon baking powder
240g / 8½oz grated carrots
4 eggs
pinch of salt
1 teaspoon vanilla essence
55g / 2oz icing sugar
70g / 2½oz honey
½ teaspoon cinnamon
2 heaped tablespoons natural
yoghurt

Preheat oven to 180°C (350°F). Grease a 23cm (9 inch) round baking tin.

Finely chop the hazelnuts. Place in a bowl with the ground almonds and mix in the baking powder and grated carrots.

Add the egg yolks, vanilla essence, icing sugar, honey, cinnamon and yoghurt. Mix until well combined.

Whip the egg whites with a pinch of salt until firm. Delicately fold into the mixture. Pour this mixture into the prepared tin and fan bake for 30 minutes. Enjoy warm or cold.

This cake makes an afternoon tea treat and is full of goodness too. It even contains a significant amount of vegetables! Hazelnuts and almonds contain iron, zinc and magnesium and are also quite high in protein so are good to include regularly into your diet. They also have a high fat content but most of this fat is unsaturated. However, some people may be allergic to nuts so always be careful when offering them to young children. Offer them alone in small quantities first to make sure they do not trigger an allergic reaction, before including them into other foods. For children under the age of one, substitute the honey with sugar.

Délice de yaourt

Yoghurt berry delight

Makes 4

Ingredients

240g / 8½oz fresh strawberries
1 x 410g / 1 x 14½oz tin of
raspberries in syrup
1 small meringue
1 tablespoon icing sugar
600g / 1lb 5oz Greek-style yoghurt
1 teaspoon vanilla bean paste
4 mint leaves

Drain the raspberries and divide between
four glasses. Crush the meringue and
use to cover the raspberries. Hull the
strawberries. Set four aside and cut the
rest into pieces. Divide the strawberry
pieces evenly between the four glasses
and place over the crushed meringue.

Mix the yoghurt with the vanilla bean
paste and icing sugar. Use to cover
the berry mixture. Use the reserved
strawberries and the mint leaves to
garnish. Serve chilled.

This pretty dessert is sweet and truly indulgent. Quick to make it also provides fibre and vitamin C. It is fresh and perfect in the summer months when berries are in season.

Milkshake au soja

Soy milkshake

Makes 4 x 200ml (7fl oz) glasses

Ingredients

300g / 10½oz fresh strawberries
1 banana
2 tablespoons raspberry syrup
1 tablespoon vanilla sugar
250ml / 9fl oz soy milk, refrigerated

Hull the strawberries and place in a mixing bowl with the slices of banana and the raspberry syrup. Sprinkle with vanilla sugar and process into a smooth purée with an electric blender.

Add the soy milk and blend again. Pour into four glasses and serve chilled, with a straw to avoid spilling.

Sometimes the best way to get a child to eat a certain fruit is to juice it, or to blend it in a milkshake. This is just what I have done here. This milkshake has a smooth texture and gets its sweetness mainly from the fruit. Soy milk is a good alternative for people who have a dairy-free diet and is made from soy beans, one of the few plant sources of complete protein. If you can't find vanilla sugar, substitute with the same amount of icing sugar and one teaspoon vanilla essence. To make your own vanilla sugar, split a vanilla pod lengthways and scrape the seeds out into a bowl. Mix in 500g / 1lb 2oz white sugar, add the vanilla pod and mix well. Transfer to an airtight container and leave for at least two weeks. Use in small quantities to give a sweet vanilla flavour to cakes and desserts.

Piles de pommes à la cannelle

Cinnamon and apple stacks

Makes 4

Ingredients

2 apples
15g / ½oz butter
1 teaspoon ground cinnamon
1 tablespoon honey
4 sheets filo pastry
1 egg yolk
1 tablespoon milk
2 strawberries

Preheat oven to 200°C (400°F). Grease an ovenproof tray. Peel and slice the apples. Place in a frying pan with the butter and cinnamon and cook for 10 minutes or until tender. Remove from the heat and mix in the honey.

Stack the sheets of filo pastry and cut into four strips along the smallest side. Cut each strip into three pieces. Place these twelve pieces of pastry on the prepared tray. Mix the egg yolk with the milk and use to brush the top of each piece of filo pastry. Fan bake for 10 minutes or until crispy and golden.

Place four pieces of the prepared filo pastry on four dessert plates. Divide half the slices of apples to cover each piece. Top with another piece of cooked pastry and repeat. Top with the remaining four pieces of filo pastry and garnish with half a strawberry. Serve with a dollop of natural yoghurt.

This dessert looks attractive and will suit adults just as much as children. Children love layering their food … and often enjoy decomposing it to eat it one layer at a time. Filo pastry is virtually fat-free and is a much healthier option than puff pastry. The apples are cooked with cinnamon and honey to make them tender and tasty. Once assembled with the crunchy pastry, they become the most wonderful way to end a meal. For children under the age of one, substitute the honey with sugar or omit altogether.

Bouchées aux myrtilles

One-bite blueberry cakes

Makes 12

Ingredients

3 eggs
1 tablespoon vanilla sugar
55g / 2oz liquid honey
55g / 2oz flour
1 teaspoon baking powder
100g / 3½oz fresh blueberries

Preheat oven to 180ºC (350ºF). Grease a mini-muffin tin.

Put the eggs with the sugar and honey in a bowl placed over a saucepan filled with simmering water. Whisk for five minutes or until warm.

Remove from the heat and whisk the mixture until cool. Mix in the flour and baking powder and beat until well combined.

Pour this mixture into the prepared tin and scatter with the blueberries. Fan bake for 20 minutes and enjoy warm or cold, dusted with icing sugar.

I will never say it enough. I love blueberries. My oldest daughter shares my enthusiasm but her younger sister does not. So it was great to see her eat some of the fruit we had been picking together once they were mixed with other ingredients and baked. Of course, it helped that we made these cute little cakes together, as children always enjoy tasting their own creations. Blueberries are a good source of vitamin C and a fruit you do not want to miss out on during the relatively short summer season. For children under the age of one, substitute the honey with sugar.

Salade de fruits

Spicy dried fruit salad

Serves 6

Ingredients

> 2 apples
> 10 pitted dried prunes
> 10 dried apricots
> 6 stoned dates
> 6 dried figs
> 15g / ½oz butter
> ½ lemon
> pinch of ground mixed spices
> pinch of ground nutmeg
> 1 whole clove
> 1 cinnamon stick

Peel and slice the apples. Cut the apricots, prunes, dates and figs into small pieces.

Place all the fruit in a frying pan along with the butter. Sprinkle with the mixed spices and nutmeg. Add the whole clove, cinnamon stick and cook over medium heat for 15 minutes, mixing the fruit once in a while.

Remove the clove and cinnamon stick. Divide between six cups and serve warm, with a dollop of natural yoghurt if desired.

Many children enjoy eating dried fruit as a snack. They are a healthy food choice too. In addition to containing many minerals such as iron, manganese and potassium, they are naturally sweet and do not require the addition of any sugar. Cook them and they quickly regain their tenderness and moisture, and become different. Not quite like fresh fruit, but not quite like dried fruit as we know them either.

Muësli

Bircher muesli

Serves 4

Ingredients

- 55g / 2oz dried apricots
- 5 dried figs
- 70g / 2½oz rolled oats
- 30g / 1oz sultanas
- ½ apple, grated
- 3 heaped tablespoons Greek-style yoghurt
- 250ml / 9fl oz apple juice
- 125g / 4½oz seedless grapes

Cut the dried apricots and figs into small pieces. Place the oats in a mixing bowl. Mix in the sultanas, grated apple, dried figs and apricot pieces. Add the yoghurt and mix well. Cover with apple juice and leave in the fridge overnight.

Divide the mixture between four cereal bowls and top with the halved grapes. Serve as a healthy and nutritious breakfast.

This traditional Swiss muesli is loved all over the world and there are many recipes for it. In this version, I used a variety of dried fruit, fresh fruit and fruit juice as well as some thick and creamy Greek-style yoghurt. The sweetness of the fruit takes away the need to add any sugar. This muesli makes a nutritious and flavoursome breakfast – a welcome change from the traditional toast or bowl of cereals. The apple juice may be substituted with any other flavour of your choice. If allergy is not an issue and depending on the children's age, you may also wish to add roughly chopped almonds, hazelnuts and walnuts.

Biscuits à la farine d'avoine

Oatmeal people

Makes 6

Ingredients

- 55g / 2oz oatmeal
- 70g / 2½oz wholemeal flour
- 30g / 1oz ground almonds
- 1 teaspoon baking powder
- 70g / 2½oz butter
- 2 tablespoons milk
- 3 tablespoons honey
- 30g / 1oz dark chocolate

Preheat oven to 180°C (350°F). Grease a 35 x 27cm (14 x 11 inch) biscuit tray.

Mix the oatmeal, wholemeal flour, ground almonds and baking powder in a bowl. Add the melted butter, milk and honey. Combine into a paste.

Place spoonfuls of this mixture onto the prepared tray. Use your fingers to shape the biscuits into people. Bake for 12 to 15 minutes and leave to cool.

Melt the chocolate with a few drops of water and use to make eyes, nose and mouth. If desired, use silver balls to decorate.

Children just love biscuits shaped into people or animals. Decorate them with a few silver balls and some chocolate and they become a guaranteed hit. Made with wholemeal flour and oatmeal, these biscuits contain useful amounts of fibre and protein. For children under the age of one, substitute the honey with sugar.

Family Meals

Bringing the family together

Mealtimes make wonderful opportunities to get the whole family sitting together around the table and sharing in their day's experiences. Of course, when children are very young it can be rather tricky to get the whole family eating together. My husband and I often find it hard to actually sit down to a meal when our children need help and supervision with their food. When the baby decides that he wants a breastfeed just as I am about to have my first mouthful (as babies do), it becomes impossible. And of course children's evening routine and bed times might make it a challenge to have dinner together in the early years.

But still, I believe it is good practice to try and make the effort to sit together for a meal whenever possible. Children are more likely to want to try new foods if they see you eating them. This makes eating together a good opportunity to achieve diversity in your children's diet, which is crucial in forming healthy lifelong eating habits.

Tips

If you are planning to eat with your children, either occasionally or all the time, make sure to have food ready at their usual mealtime to ensure as little stress as possible. If you wait for them to get overly hungry or tired they are likely to be irritable and difficult to manage…not a great combination for a pleasant meal. Try to keep mealtimes regular and predictable. It is much better to sit down to a proper meal three times a day than to snack constantly throughout the day. Having regular and planned meals also removes the need to use convenience food, and will stop your children from eating erratically.

If the prospect of a whole meal with your preschoolers is overwhelming, you could try sitting down with the kids to help them eat their main dish first. It will allow you to have yours in peace once their hunger is under control (here's hoping!). You can then all enjoy sharing dessert together. This works well for us. Small children don't have the attention span to sit through a lengthy meal, but just sitting down for dessert together has become a ritual during the weekend that everybody in our family looks forward to.

To make a shared meal successful, start by making sure you include at least one healthy food that you know your children enjoy. This way, they won't be turned off by what is on the table. To make the meal more interesting and appetising to your children, include different colours and textures. Invest in dinnerware that is appropriate for preschoolers. Colourful plasticware is fun, almost unbreakable, and fairly cheap.

Accept that children behave like children, so don't expect impeccable table manners. They learn from you, but there is a learning curve and perfect manners do not happen right away. Having said that, do encourage them to behave in an appropriate way and to ask for food or drinks politely.

Do not allow them to bring toys or games to the table. Young children are easily distracted and may not sit still for very long, so you need to eliminate obvious distractions. When you are eating together as a family, switch the television off. Mealtimes make great opportunities to catch up and share each other's day and experiences. Watching TV takes this option away. Moreover, being distracted leads to gobbling food down without really appreciating it, and often to eating less nutritious foods in larger quantities.

Last but not least, try to always keep your cool. This may be difficult when you are tired and have spent time preparing a meal that remains almost entirely untouched. But keeping calm will stop your children from creating a negative association with food. Make the most of shared meals to teach your children good eating habits that will last a lifetime.

Riz au lait

Fruity rice pudding

Serves 4

Ingredients

- 125g / 4½oz short-grain rice
- 500ml / 18fl oz milk
- 55g / 2oz sugar
- 1 teaspoon vanilla essence
- 1 x 410g / 1 x 14½oz tin apricot halves in juice

Raspberry coulis

- 1 x 410g / 1 x 14½oz tin raspberries in syrup
- 1 lemon
- 2 tablespoons icing sugar

To make the raspberry coulis drain the raspberries, setting aside four tablespoons of the syrup. Mix the fruit in a food processor, pass through a sieve and collect the seedless purée in a bowl. Add the lemon juice, icing sugar and the reserved syrup and mix until smooth.

To make the vanilla creamed rice, place the milk in a saucepan with the rice and cook over low heat for 30 to 40 minutes until all the milk has been absorbed and the rice is tender. Stir occasionally, adding a little extra milk if necessary. Mix in the sugar and vanilla essence. Drain the apricot halves and cut into small pieces.

To assemble, divide the apricot pieces between four ice-cream cups. Add a little apricot juice and cover with some vanilla creamed rice. Top with some raspberry coulis and serve chilled.

This dessert combines a mixture of fruit, starchy carbohydrates and dairy. This makes it a very wholesome dessert, snack or breakfast. It can also be made in a very short time by using ready-made creamed rice. For an express version of this dessert, use 1 x 400g / 1 x 14oz vanilla creamed rice. For convenience, I have used tinned fruit but fresh seasonal fruit can be used instead. Many of the qualities of the food are retained in tinned food and although fresh is always best, this can be a good alternative when time is lacking. This makes a great pudding all year round.

Crumble aux fruits

Fruit crumble

Serves 4

Ingredients

    6 dried apricots
    40g / 1½oz sultanas
    2 apples
    1 x 410g / 1 x 14½oz tin pear slices in juice
    40g / 1½oz rolled oats
    40g / 1½oz ground almonds
    40g / 1½oz butter
    1 teaspoon raw sugar

Preheat oven to 180°C (350°F). Grease a 20cm (8 inch) round baking tin.

Peel and slice the apples. Drain the pears. Place at the bottom of the prepared tin along with the sultanas and the chopped apricots.

Mix the rolled oats, ground almonds and melted butter together. Use to top the fruit and sprinkle with raw sugar. Fan bake for 35 minutes. Divide between four dessert bowls and enjoy warm with a glass of milk.

Crumble is one of my favourite desserts and it can be made with so many different fruit. In this recipe I mixed fresh fruit with dried fruit and tinned fruit. I also used ground almonds and rolled oats in the topping. Both are sources of unsaturated fat.

Petit déj liquide tout en un

Makes 2 × 200ml (7 fl oz) glasses

Ingredients

   1 banana
   100ml / 3½fl oz freshly squeezed orange juice
   2 tablespoons oats
   3 tablespoons Greek-style yoghurt
   1 tablespoon liquid honey
   1 tablespoon chocolate hail

Peel and slice the banana.

Place all the ingredients except for the chocolate hail into a mixing bowl and blend with an electric mixer until frothy.

Pour into two glasses and sprinkle with the chocolate hail. Serve chilled with a few slices of banana.

This smoothie can be a good substitute to solid food and can make a yummy liquid breakfast if your children are just not hungry in the morning. It is nutritious and contains among other things vitamin C, potassium and calcium. Quick to make, it can be prepared even on a busy morning. The texture of this smoothie is quite thick so it can be eaten with a spoon. To make it runnier, add a little milk and sip with a straw. Depending on the season, you can vary the flavours and add some berries or other fruit of your choice. For children under the age of one, substitute the honey with sugar or omit altogether.

Cookies au chocolat

Chocolate cookies

Makes 12

Ingredients

125g / 4½oz unsalted butter
125g / 4½oz sweetened condensed milk
1 egg
70g / 2½oz brown sugar
150g / 5½oz flour
70g / 2½oz dark chocolate chips

Preheat oven to 180ºC (350ºF). Grease a 35 x 27cm (14 x 11 inch) biscuit tray.

Melt the butter. Mix in the condensed milk. Beat in the egg and brown sugar and mix until well combined. Add the flour. Lastly, mix in the chocolate chips.

Place spoonfuls of this mixture onto the prepared tray, leaving enough room between each as the cookies will spread while baking. Fan bake for 15 to 20 minutes. Remove from the tray and leave to cool on a rack. Alternatively, spread the mixture all over the tray and cut out into various shapes once baked.

Let's face it, these cookies are scrumptious and decadent. But realistically, who would want to stop their children from enjoying such a treat once in a while? Serve them at a party or for a special afternoon tea with a glass of milk. Your children will love you for it.

Safety

Allergies and intolerances

It is estimated that between five and eight per cent of children have a food allergy. An allergy is an overreaction to a substance that, for most of us, is harmless. Symptoms of an allergic reaction can include:

- Chest tightness
- Skin rashes or eczema
- Runny nose
- Itchy eyes
- Vomiting and diarrhoea
- Swelling of the lips, palate, tongue, or throat
- Sleep disorders

These reactions typically occur anywhere between a few minutes to two hours after the food which caused the allergic reaction is ingested.

Food intolerances are more common and are not as serious as allergies. A food intolerance occurs when a food irritates the digestive system, or cannot be digested. Food

intolerances can have unpleasant or painful symptoms, but they are not life-threatening because they do not trigger the immune responses that allergies cause.

The incidence of allergies has significantly increased in the past 25 years. This may be linked to a number of factors including nutrition and lifestyle. Many allergies are found in babies and children with no family history.

Most allergic reactions in children are caused by cow's milk, soy, eggs, nuts, gluten, fish, and shellfish. Children often outgrow allergies to the first three, but allergies to the other foods listed generally last into adulthood. The first two years are critical as this is when a toddler's diet can help protect him against allergies later in life.

Choking

Choking can also be a problem with young children. Here are a few tips to help prevent it from happening:

- Always stay with your preschoolers while they are eating so you can act immediately if they run into trouble.
- Tell your children to chew well and show them how you do it.
- Teach your children not to overfill their mouths.
- Avoid drinking and eating at the same time.
- Do not let your children run or play while they are eating.
- Do not force-feed a child, especially one who is laughing, crying, or upset.

Food safety

When it comes to food safety, there are some basic guidelines to follow:

- Wash your hands before preparing food.
- Wash your hands before each meal, and teach your children to do the same.
- Ensure that chilled food is stored at an appropriate temperature.
- Store cooked and raw foods separately.
- Reheat cooked meals thoroughly (especially those containing meat or fish).
- Wash fruit and vegetables before eating.

These measures are not very time-consuming and can help prevent nasty tummy bugs.

Yaourt fruité

Homemade fruit yoghurt

Serves 4

Ingredients

- 240g / 8½oz natural yoghurt
- 100g / 3½oz Greek-style yoghurt
- 55g / 2oz sugar
- 1 teaspoon vanilla essence
- 6 apricots
- 2 peaches
- 4 glacé cherries
- 2 tablespoons passion fruit syrup

Halve and stone the apricots. Peel, halve and stone the peaches. Cut two apricots halves and one peach half into pieces.

Place the remaining peach and apricot halves, natural yoghurt, Greek-style yoghurt, sugar and vanilla essence in a bowl. Process into a smooth purée with an electric blender.

Divide the fruit yoghurt between four bowls. Top with the reserved fruit pieces, glacé cherries and passion fruit syrup. Serve chilled.

Fruit yoghurt tastes delicious but all too often, the ready-made variety is full of colourings, flavourings and other rather unnatural sounding ingredients. Not to mention the amount of added sugar is often more than what is needed while the amount of actual fresh fruit used can be rather lacking. This is why making your own fruit yoghurt can be a good alternative. Try it with various fruit depending on the season and use good quality plain yoghurt as a base.

Pain perdu

Vanilla bread pudding

Serves 4

Ingredients

4 slices bread
1 apple
55g / 2oz sultanas
12 pitted dried prunes
4 eggs
280ml / 10fl oz milk
1 teaspoon vanilla bean paste
2 tablespoons vanilla sugar
1 teaspoon raw sugar

Preheat oven to 180°C (350°F). Remove the crust from the slices of bread and place at the bottom of a 20 x 20cm (9 x 9 inch) square baking dish.

Peel and slice the apple. Scatter the sultanas, prunes and slices of apple over the bread.

Whisk the eggs with the milk, vanilla bean paste and vanilla sugar. Pour over the bread. Sprinkle with the raw sugar and bake for 20 minutes or until golden. Serve warm for dessert or afternoon tea.

This is a classic pudding to which I have added a good dose of fruit. It provides calcium, proteins and vitamins and adds a sweet touch at the end of a meal. Vanilla bean paste and vanilla sugar can be bought from the supermarket. If preferred, they can be replaced with natural vanilla essence.

Biscuits aux épices

Makes 15

Ingredients

> 80g / 3oz butter
> 2 tablespoons honey
> 80g / 3oz raw sugar
> 2 eggs
> 1 teaspoon vanilla essence
> 230g / 8oz wholemeal flour
> 1 teaspoon baking powder
> 1 teaspoon ground ginger
> 1 teaspoon ground mixed spices
> silver balls and hundreds and
> thousands to decorate

Preheat oven to 180°C (350°F). Grease a 35 x 27cm (14 x 11 inch) biscuit tray.

Mix the melted butter, honey and raw sugar together. Beat in the eggs and vanilla essence. Fold in the wholemeal flour, baking powder, ground ginger and ground mixed spices. Mix until well combined.

Spread this mixture into the prepared tin and bake for 20 minutes. Cut out into different shapes and press silver balls and hundreds and thousands into each biscuit to decorate. Enjoy warm or cold, with a glass of milk.

Nothing beats homemade biscuits. They taste delicious and are so convenient to put in your bag when you are on the go. The combination of spices gives these ones a wonderful flavour. I have used raw sugar, honey and wholemeal flour to make the most of natural ingredients which are not over-processed. For children under the age of one, substitute the honey with sugar or omit altogether.

Petits gâteaux au yaourt

Yoghurt cupcakes

Makes 15

Ingredients

500g / 1lb 2oz Greek-style yoghurt
100g / 3½oz sugar
1 teaspoon vanilla bean paste
4 eggs
zest of 1 lemon
55g / 2oz corn flour
2 ripe peaches
a few strawberries

Preheat oven to 160°C (325°F). Grease a mini-muffin baking tin or use silicon bakeware that does not require greasing.

Mix the yoghurt, sugar and vanilla bean paste together. Beat in the eggs and the zest of the lemon. Fold in the corn flour.

Peel, stone and cut the peaches into small pieces and add to the mixture.

Pour into the prepared tin. Bake for 30 minutes or until just set. Serve chilled with a few fresh strawberries.

These little cakes are perfect for afternoon tea. Low in fat and with just the right amount of sugar, they can be enjoyed guilt-free by your kids. Chances are you will have trouble resisting them too! Using silicon bakeware saves from using fat and makes removing food from the tin and doing the dishes a whole lot easier. It has become my bakeware of choice and to my husband's delight (he often gets elected to do the dishes), it has pretty much replaced the traditional tins I used to use.

Entremets aux fruits

Fruit trifle

Serves 4

Ingredients

100g / 3½oz plain sponge
4 tablespoons orange juice
300g / 10½oz Greek-style yoghurt
½ lemon
30g / 1oz vanilla sugar
125g / 4½oz strawberries
a handful blueberries

Crumb the sponge and divide between four dessert bowls. Pour the orange juice on top. Hull the strawberries and cut into pieces. Divide between the bowls.

Mix the yoghurt with the zest and juice of the lemon. Add the sugar and mix well.

Pour the yoghurt mixture over the sponge. Decorate with a few blueberries if desired and serve chilled.

This dessert can be made in many different ways. Choose fresh fruit depending on the season. No fuss and bake-free, this recipe is ideal to make when you have little time to spare in the kitchen. For a special treat, add a layer of homemade custard.

Barres de céréales aux fruits

Cereal bars

Makes 15

Ingredients

240g / 8½oz rolled oats
30g / 1oz sultanas
10 stoned dates
12 dried apricots
1 tablespoon golden syrup
15g / ½oz muscovado sugar
175g / 6oz butter

Preheat oven to 180°C (350°F). Grease a 35 x 27cm (14 x 11 inch) biscuit tray.

Cut the dates and apricots into pieces. Mix the rolled oats with the sultanas, dates and apricots. Add the golden syrup, muscovado sugar and melted butter and combine well.

Spread this mixture over the tray and bake for 20 minutes or until golden. Cut into rectangles and use as a nutritious snack on the go.

Sweet, tasty and nutritious these cereal bars are just perfect for busy kids who need lots of energy. Offer them as a snack, or pack them in a lunchbox for an older child. They are easy to make and I personally prefer making my own than buying ready-made cereal bars from the shops as they are cheaper and tastier and do not contain any additives. These cereal bars can be kept for up to two weeks in an airtight container.

Crème brûlée à la papaye

Pawpaw brulée

Makes 4

Ingredients

600g / 1lb 5oz Greek-style yoghurt
1 tablespoon vanilla sugar
1 pawpaw
½ lemon, juiced
30g / 1oz icing sugar
4 teaspoons raw sugar

Preheat oven to 220°C (425°F). Beat the yoghurt with the vanilla sugar. Halve the pawpaw and remove the seeds. Spoon out the flesh. Add to the yoghurt and drizzle with lemon juice. Process with an electric blender. Divide between four individual ovenproof dishes.

Sprinkle each dish with one teaspoon raw sugar and put in the oven under the grill for a few minutes or until the sugar has melted. Serve immediately.

It can sometimes be difficult to get a child to eat an apple or a banana – what are the chances that they will have exotic fruit? Well, the answer may be to hide it away! By blending the pawpaw with some creamy vanilla-flavoured yoghurt, your children will not even realize they have been so adventurous. As an ad for a famous French company selling tinned vegetables went, "By the time I realized it was too late… I had already enjoyed my meal."

Tartelettes de filo

Filo tartlets

Makes 4

Ingredients

- 4 sheets filo pastry
- 1 egg yolk
- 1 tablespoon milk
- 1 banana
- 100g / 3½oz cream cheese
- 100g / 3½oz natural yoghurt
- 1 teaspoon vanilla bean paste
- 2 tablespoons liquid honey
- 2 tablespoons raw sugar
- 4 strawberries
- 1 kiwi fruit

Preheat oven to 180°C (350°F). Fold each sheet of filo pastry into four and place each one at the bottom of an individual greased baking tin. Mix the egg yolk with the milk and use to lightly brush the sides of the pastry. Bake for 10 minutes or until crispy and golden.

Slice the banana and divide between the tartlets. Process the cream cheese, yoghurt, vanilla bean paste, honey and raw sugar together until smooth. Use to cover the slices of banana.

Hull and slice the strawberries. Peel and slice the kiwi fruit. Top each tartlet with slices of strawberries and kiwi fruit.

These crispy little tartlets will be a hit. Make sure to add the filling just before serving as it will make the filo pastry go soggy if added too long in advance. You can garnish the top of the tartlets with any fruit your children enjoy, and even throw in some chocolate hail if it is for a special occasion! The vanilla bean paste may be substituted for natural vanilla essence. For children under the age of one, substitute the honey with sugar or omit altogether.

Mousse au citron

Lemon mousse

Serves 4

Ingredients

300g / 10½oz Greek-style yoghurt
2 lemons
40g / 2½oz icing sugar
70g / 2½oz sweetened condensed milk
2 egg whites
pinch of salt

Beat the yoghurt with the juice of the lemons and the icing sugar. Mix in the condensed milk.

Whip the egg whites with a pinch of salt until firm. Fold delicately into the yoghurt mixture.

Divide evenly between four dessert bowls. Serve chilled, garnished with lemon rind or berry fruit purée if desired.

Lemon mousse has to be one of my favourite desserts. Full of calcium and vitamin C, this particular recipe is very simple and takes very little time to prepare. Just refrigerate and serve chilled.

Smoothie sans laitage

Dairy-free smoothie

Makes 4 x 250ml (9 fl oz) glasses

Ingredients

- 300g / 10½oz silken tofu
- 1 banana
- 240g / 8½oz blueberries
- 450ml / 16fl oz soy milk
- 200ml / 7fl oz freshly squeezed orange juice
- 4 tablespoons liquid honey

Peel and slice the banana. Wash and dry the blueberries.

Place all the ingredients in a mixing bowl and blend with an electric mixer. Pour into four tall glasses and serve chilled.

Smoothies are always favoured by children who love a special drink served with a straw. Colourful and creamy, this smoothie provides potassium as well as vitamin C and protein. It is sweet enough just through the use of ripe fruit and is made in a matter of minutes.

Exercise

Get moving

Exercise helps young children to improve their coordination, balance, and posture. Exercising regularly also speeds up the metabolism and significantly reduces a child's risk of becoming overweight. It is not healthy or comfortable for children (or adults) to be overweight. As well as the physical risks, overweight children may be bullied or teased at school.

Exercise helps develop strong bones and muscles as well as a healthy heart, lungs, and arteries. Additional benefits include a lower risk of heart disease, diabetes, and even some cancers later in life. You don't need to enrol your children in every possible sports club to get them moving. Preschoolers do not need much incentive to go off and play energetically. In fact, it can be quite hard to stop them from running around!

Avoid letting children spend too much time in front of the TV or computer. The more time spent in front of a screen, the less time there is left for physical activity and play. Of course, I am the first person to acknowledge that DVDs can be very useful while juggling several young children, housework, and a day job or a home business. But their use should be limited. Refrain from giving your children crisps or sweets while they are lying on the sofa watching TV. This must be the quickest way to obesity and is not a healthy habit. Instead, set a time limit and offer water and slices of fruit or another healthy snack if they feel hungry (see page 18 for ideas). They will thank you for it some time down the track!

Be involved

Playgrounds are a great place to let off some steam and interact with other children. Encourage your littlies to spend their energy in a physical way and to go and play outside whenever possible. They will enjoy such outings even more if you take part. Things as simple as a skipping rope provide endless possibilities for physical games.

We have regular fun activities at home where the children and I do gymnastics or dance energetically. The upside is that we can do this just as well in the garden as in the lounge if the weather is not so good. It is also a time filled with shrieking laughter and another way for me to bond with them.

Seeing you being active is also a sure way to get your children interested in sports. My husband regularly goes running with a child in the buggy, or inline-skating with all three of them in the buggy. The kids just love it, keep asking for more, and can't wait to go running with dad themselves. As for me, I somehow manage to swim every day and make sure to take each child with me once a week. I also love biking, so whenever possible I make this outing with mum even more special by including a bike ride, a swim and a snack, plus some time having fun in the playground next to the swimming pool. Each child looks forward to it and so do I!

Gâteau à la banane

Banana cake

Serves 8

Ingredients

- 2 eggs
- 55g / 2oz light muscovado sugar
- 125g / 4½oz butter
- 2 ripe bananas
- 100g / 3½oz white flour
- 55g / 2oz rye flour
- 1 teaspoon cinnamon
- 1 tablespoon baking powder
- icing sugar to dust

Preheat oven to 160°C (325°F). Grease a 23 × 12cm (9 × 5 inch) loaf tin.

Beat the eggs with the muscovado sugar and add the melted butter. Mix until well combined. Purée the bananas with a fork and add to the mixture.

Beat in the white flour, rye flour, cinnamon and baking powder. Pour into the prepared tin and fan bake for 30 minutes or until a fine skewer or toothpick inserted into the centre of the cake comes out clean. Dust with icing sugar and serve with a few slices of banana.

A traditional afternoon tea treat, this cake can be sliced and taken on a picnic, put in a lunchbox or in your bag when you are out and about with the children. It will keep them going and the use of rye flour and bananas contributes to making it a healthy snacking option. For children under the age of one, substitute the honey with sugar or omit altogether.

CONVERSION TABLES

The following amounts have been rounded up or down for convenience. All have been kitchen tested. All the recipe baking times are based on a fan oven.

Metric to imperial

15g ½oz	30ml 1fl oz
30g 1oz	55ml 2fl oz
40g 1½oz	75ml 3fl oz
55g 2oz	100ml 3½fl oz
70g 2½oz	120ml 4fl oz
80g 3oz	150ml 5fl oz
100g 3½oz	155ml 5½fl oz
125g 4½oz	200ml 7fl oz
140g 5oz	225ml 8fl oz
150g 5½oz	250ml 9fl oz
175g 6oz	280ml 10fl oz (½ pint)
200g 7oz	330ml 12fl oz
210g 7½oz	400ml 14fl oz
230g 8oz	500ml 18fl oz
240g 8½oz	555ml 20fl oz (1 pint)
275g 9½oz	600ml 22fl oz
300g 10½oz	750ml 27fl oz
360g 12½oz	1 litre 34fl oz (1¾ pint)
375g 13oz	1¼ litre 2¼ pints
400g 14oz	1½ litre 2½ pints
450g 1lb	2 litres 3¼ pints
500g 1lb 2oz	
600g 1lb 5oz	
700g 1lb 8oz	
750g 1lb 10oz	
800g 1lb 12oz	
1kg 2lb 3oz	

Cups to metric and imperial

	1 cup	½ cup	¼ cup
Flour	125g / 4½oz	55g / 2oz	30g / 1oz
Sugar	150g / 5½oz	80g / 3oz	20g / ¾oz
Desiccated coconut	80g / 3oz	40g / 1½oz	40g / 1½oz
Ground almonds	100g / 3½oz	50g / 2oz	30g / 1oz
Walnut pieces	80g / 3oz	40g / 1½oz	20g / ¾oz
Yoghurt	200g / 7oz	100g / 3½oz	55g / 2oz
Milk	250ml / 8½fl oz	120ml / 4fl oz	55ml / 2fl oz
Fresh cream	250ml / 8½fl oz	120ml / 4fl oz	55ml / 2fl oz
Water	250ml / 8½fl oz	120ml / 4fl oz	55ml / 2fl oz

Oven temperatures

120°C	250°F	Gas mark 1
150°C	300°F	Gas mark 2
160°C	325°F	Gas mark 3
180°C	350°F	Gas mark 4
190°C	375°F	Gas mark 5
200°C	400°F	Gas mark 6
220°C	425°F	Gas mark 7

Baking tins

Common square and rectangular baking tin sizes	
20 x 20cm	8 x 8 inch
23 x 12cm	9 x 5 inch
35 x 27cm	14 x 11 inch
Common round baking tin sizes	
18cm	7 inch
21cm	8 inch
23cm	9 inch
25cm	10 inch

INDEX

ACKNOWLEDGEMENTS

First of all, I would like to thank Sue Pollard from the New Zealand Nutrition Foundation for her supportive comments and feedback on my book. Many thanks also to Victoria Landells for kindly accepting to review all my recipes and the nutritional information printed in this book, as well as for writing the foreword to this book. Vic, your professional knowledge of the health and nutrition sector has been invaluable.

I would like to make a special mention of my photography tutor, famous photographer and book author, Tony Bridge. Tony, without your help I would not have been able to take all the photographs needed for this book. I appreciate your patience and encouragements while teaching a novice like myself. Learning this new set of skills has opened new opportunities for me and I will always be grateful for this.

I would also like to acknowledge the work of my incredibly talented graphic designer friend, Vanessa Jones. Vanessa, you once again produced a work of the highest quality. I feel privileged to work with you and delighted that we were able to continue our partnership despite now living on either sides of the Tasman. Claire Collier, many thanks for taking the time to edit my text. Thanks also to Andrew Tizzard, my book distributor, for your feedback and advice on this book. Last but not least, a special thanks to my husband for his constant support, and to my lovely children for taking on the roles of models as well as guinea pigs for this book!

CHRISTELLE LE RU

Christelle was born in France in 1975 and graduated as an electrical and software engineer in 1997. After five years of working in France and the UK, Christelle and her husband moved to New Zealand, a country that represented everything they were looking for. They settled in Christchurch in 2002 and became New Zealand citizens in 2006. Mid-2008 Christelle gave up her day job as a software engineer to fully focus on her small children, Noémie, Éloïse and Yohann, and food writing. An award-winning author and publisher, she is also a food columnist for various publications and produces her own food photography. An active woman, she keeps fit with daily bike rides and swims.

Ever since she was young, Christelle has taken great pleasure in cooking and baking for her family and friends. She puts her passion for good food down to her mum, who she thinks is the best cook ever. Christelle loves experimenting in the kitchen, and delights in the art of creating new dishes. Yet her approach to cooking is down-to-earth, and her recipes are easily accessible by the home cook.

Her first book, *Simply Irresistible French Desserts*, was an award-winning collection of her favourite desserts. *French Fare* won an award for Best French Cuisine cookbook at the Gourmand World Cookbook Awards while *Passion Chocolat* received an award in the Best Chocolate book category. *Fresh Start* is Christelle's fourth cookbook and reflects her focus as a mum to give her children a taste for a healthy lifestyle and nutritious foods from an early age.